The Cobbled Path

The Cobbled Path

Reflections and Thoughts

Patrick Webber

JANUS PUBLISHING COMPANY
London, England

First published in Great Britain 2008
by Janus Publishing Company Ltd,
105-107 Gloucester Place,
London W1U 6BY

www.januspublishing.co.uk

British Library Cataloguing-in-Publication Data
A catalogue record for this book is available from the British Library

ISBN 978-1-85756-619-2

Cover Design: Kevin Mwangi

Printed and bound in Great Britain

This book is dedicated with love to my children:
Patrick, Chelsie-Louisa, Kyle and Calum,
who inspire me daily!
And who are in every beat of my heart.

Also, to all of those people who have made my yesterdays, having
played a part in getting me here today, and who will help me
to arrive at the as yet unforeseen tomorrow.

About The Author

I am a thirty-eight-year-old sufferer of Primary Progressive Multiple Sclerosis (MS); as such, I am unable to work any more. I served in the British Army for five years, after which I almost enlisted in the French Foreign Legion, but was lucky enough to be allowed to leave le Citadel, in the town of Lille, before it was too late. I hold Black Belts in three disciplines of the martial arts, Taekwondo, Freestyle Karate and Kick-Boxing, and became the Chief Instructor for Koryo Kick-Boxing, an amalgamation of all three disciplines, gaining the coveted rank/grade of Master: I lived and breathed health and fitness, managing to reach a high level of facility management both here in the United Kingdom and abroad in the Middle East, where I also became the personal trainer to a member of a North African royal family. In hindsight, I was unwise to make the leisure industry the centre of my world, and to put all of my eggs in to one basket. However I feel lucky enough to have achieved all of the goals throughout my life to date, which I have worked towards, and have no regrets about the choices which I have had and the decisions I have made. I met Karen whilst we were both living and working in Saudi Arabia, and we both entered into a relationship, on every level: the physical, the emotional and the spiritual, through which all of my opinions, my thought patterns and the way I lived my life changed. The metaphysics of my piece of the universe was an open book, my mind was opened up, as was my third eye, and my very consciousness found itself on a whole new path, 'my very own cobbled path', to self-discovery, and realisation. I was made aware of the need to reprioritise certain milestones which I needed to work towards and I learnt how to pigeon-hole the milestones which had already been reached. I liked the very simple, yet very powerful, concepts of good old-fashioned kindness and universal love as much as I liked, and was drawn to, the more complex underlying meaning of it all. I've always been lucky enough to be able to express my thoughts, feelings, opinions and emotions in the spoken word, but this is my first attempt at putting those words down on paper. I hope that you are able to take something from the book, a single word, a phrase, a sentence, a paragraph, or piece of work; in its entirety, makes my writing it all the more worthwhile. Most of all I hope you enjoy reading it as much as I have enjoyed writing it, and I hope it gives you food for thought, as it has me.

I feel 'aware' that 'Spirit' are near me when I am writing, and would like to acknowledge and thank them for helping me and, more often than not, guiding my hand and my thoughts.

'*The Cobbled Path* is a book for the thinker; not so much a light read, but a book to pick up on those occasions when seeking another human being's guidance into the deeper world of thought. The reader should feel that they are able to identify with certain pieces of the author's work, whilst simply enjoying it as a whole.' – Deirdre Ann Turner – published author of *Lilac Sky*

The Desert Sands

As I say goodbye to the desert sands of Saudi Arabia, I reflect upon what lessons this journey has taught me, as I've learnt from all of my journeys through life. I've learnt that the world can be a deceiving place, one willing to hide behind the mask of glitter and extravagance, behind which lies a face of sadness and loneliness, too afraid to cry out and which would rather choose to live a lie than face reality. I have also learnt something that I knew all along, but needed to be reminded of, 'all men are created equal', and the smallest of gestures can gain the trust and friendship of those that find it hard to trust, and have never known friendship. I have also learnt that the material things that we strive for are the least important; health and happiness for ourselves and others less fortunate are far more important. If I can take from these lessons and adjust my own thoughts and actions accordingly, then I do not feel that this chapter in my life will have been wasted. As I look down over the land and fly away, I know I will shed a tear for those that have touched my heart, and I know I will not forget the sands of Saudi Arabia; or those people who have no choice but to live out their lives under the raised sandal.

Maybes

Maybe if we (all religions) were called to pray,
We might get on a little better,
at least twice or three times a day!
Maybe if one language in prayer we spoke,
there would be less war, throughout our world;
and in time, would realise our hope.
Wishful thinking, I know it's true,
divided by belief, both me and you.

Across the Universe

Universal love is in everything in nature; including yourself.
Return that emotion by loving everything which is universal!

Stardust

Like walking through stardust, I float through the air;

with my arms outstretched, and with the wind in my hair.

Dreams pass me by, on the highway to sleep,

carrying fresh hope; in the secrets they keep.

I look up to the stars through the darkness of night,

to guide me back home, and into the light.

Violence Be-gets

What goes around comes around (if not down here, then almost certainly on the other side). We are, it seems, dead set on disturbing the peace, whilst we are willing to take the credit for being the defenders of it; from petty crime at street level, to acts of genocide on the larger scale. 'Retribution is the same.' Therefore, it does not matter in the long run, if our laws, our politics or other factors get in the way of justice. In the end, we are all going to the same place, but one path there, is easier than the other.

Our Song

What if our lives, so many years long;

had been nothing more than a line in a song!

Who is the singer?

For what choir do they sing?

What octave, what note or what lyric do we bring?

Will we get to hear it, when we are dead and gone?

Will the angels stand beside the gates;

and will they sing our song?

Me, Myself & I

A single drop in the ocean,

the blade of grass on which I stand,

a single oak in the forest,

a single grain of sand.

In a crowd a single face, a solitary thing, in a solitary place.

Nobody shares my thoughts, and nobody shares my dreams,

nobody shares my world, as busy as it seems.

Baht 'at

Just two strangers, met by chance one foggy day on Ilkley Moor, fate dealt them both a lucky hand - or was it luck at all?

Rags 'n' Bones: (Summertime-Rural England - 1348)

Even with all the noise the cart made,

I could still make out a child's cry,

sobbing uncontrollably,

as she waved her Dad goodbye.

Solitude

Normality is something that we don't decide,

abnormal we sometimes do,

afraid of what is deemed different,

and distant from anything new.

Screaming

Millions! No Billions! are wasted on unrealistic dreams,
so much money thrown away,
whilst our planet cry's out and our planet screams.

Make the honest choice, because honesty is always the best policy.

Tiptoe

I tried to see,
something up high,
I couldn't quite get there,
I wished I could fly.

I pulled up a chair,
for me to climb up on,
I still couldn't see anything,
or maybe it had gone.

It all became clear,
nothing much to see,
just the burke up on his tiptoes,
stood on the chair, thats me.

Take to the air,
spread you wings and fly,
you'll never know until you leave the nest,
you'll never know unless you try.

Certa Cito

Mercury the winged god was the emblem that I wore,
the Royal Corps of Signals,
the messengers of war.
Even then, 'words' were the preferred weapons of my choice,
across continents, skies and oceans,
my comrades heard my voice.

Wise people know 'things',
shrewd people know those people who know things!

Music of the sun

The ladies wove lace, on a Mediterranean morn.
The men had gone fishing, before it was dawn.
Click clack, click clack, the looms worked away.
Click clack, click clack, weaving all day.
The lace they wove, all day long,
click, clack, click clack, the weaving song.

Falling - How Hard?

One foot in front of the other,
how hard can it be,
to get to the light,
at night that I see,
what stops me from making that final leap,
into the light that I see at night,
the light that accompanies me at night as I sleep?
A leap of faith,
a trust in it all,
to go to the light and to let myself fall.

Phoenix

A black as coal, as funny as a clown,

she lifts us up when we're feeling down.

In the day she sleeps, and wants to play when it's dark.

She comes running home, when she hears a dog bark,

but we've never kept her in, she has the freedom to roam,

but she's happiest with us, she's happy when she's home.

Pocket Money Day

With my pocket money in my hand I went to the shop,

and asked for some sweets, the ones from up top.

As happy as a boy could possibly be,

I looked in the paper bag only to see,

that the shopkeeper had given the wrong sweets to me.

'Excuse me', I said but bon-bon's are not the reason that I came to your shop,

I'll swap you all of these, for a single pear drop.

Toxic

We are running out of unpolluted landfill areas, and clean rivers and oceanic beds,

in which to bury all the toxic waste, which remains after industry has finished with it.

We will be ok, as all of the poisonous contents have been put into containers,

which will not degrade until most of us are gone:

What about our children, grandchildren or great-grandchildren?

What about the wildlife, the animals, the trees and the flowers?

All because, we keep on wanting!

What's the Point of It All ?

We are all here for a reason, whether it's good, bad or as indifferent and yet impartial as our views on the subject. It may have already happened; it may happen today or tomorrow, you will never know; and neither will you feel better about having done that which it is that you came here to do; but be assured that it (you) will make a difference!

An unselfish thought; or selfless act, takes only a moment, which is otherwise wasted.

Rainbows

Richard of York gave battle in vain,

the colours of a rainbow, but what's in a name?

A scientist would call it refraction of light,

I like to think that it's a gift of sight.

It's always there after the rain,

a beautiful rainbow, but what's in a name?

When we smile, and others do the same,

that is our rainbow, but what's in a name?

Prayer is good! Prayer with conviction of faith is better!
(any prayer, and any faith)

Hope

They say that 'hope, salvation and destiny are around the next corner', but! 'Have you ever had the feeling that your life is happening inside a goldfish bowl?' Going around and around, making the same old mistakes, time and time again.

A Deeper Look

Just because we cannot explain something, it does not mean that it does not exist! Just because we cannot see something, or refuse to acknowledge its existence or presence, it does not mean that it isn't there!

Someone to Laugh With

As I walked down the high street, I caught a glimpse of him through a shop window, but when I went inside to talk to him and to say hello, he had gone. That wasn't the only time that I had seen him that day, or in the days previous to that. It was almost as though he had been following me, and documenting my each and every step. Yet there was no animosity between my stalker and I, quite the opposite in fact, which takes me back to the high street. It had been jointly decided and acknowledged, between the two of us (through thought alone), that no malice was to be directed towards one another, whether purposely or not. So why had my elusive friend and adversary disappeared? I decided to go and have a cup of coffee and try to work it out; but when I went to wash my hands, I saw him again! He was right there in front of me, in the mirror; and he was copying everything that I did: when I scowled he scowled back, when I laughed he respectively returned the emotion, and laughed with me. In the weeks, months and years ahead, I had friends, who came and went, but there was always one constant in my life, and he was always there to talk to and to laugh with.

The letter was written and the ink had dried,
sealed with a smudge; from where I had cried.

What You Can't See Can't Hurt You

He was the scruffiest kid on the estate, with muck on his face, potatoes growing behind his ears, and what could easily have been mistaken for a bird's nest growing on the top of his head. Joshua, or Josh, as he liked to be called, was a bit of a loner; but for some reason, (which he could not work out) he was popular with all the other kids. Maybe because he was representative of how they would like to be, in their nicely ironed playing-out clothes, and their slick side partings, mirroring that of their mums' and their dads' personalities, and restrictions, made by their social environment; unable to break free from the mould of normality like Josh had – the epitome of scruffy little urchins, in every street and every town, up and down the country. 'Did you have a nice day at school?' his mum shouted from the living room. 'Yes thanks,' Josh replied, as he threw his bag and coat in a pile on the floor, under the coat hooks! On the way up to his room, Josh thought to himself, what kind of a question is that to ask a ten-year-old kid? She must be going mad or maybe she's going senile; I'll have to keep an eye on her, especially in the kitchen. So Josh quickly changed out of his school uniform, and left it in a nice heap on the floor, to go into the washing machine. And as though by magic, they would be returned to his wardrobe, all fresh, nicely hung and ironed, leaving Josh feeling slightly annoyed, as he had spent all week making them mucky, and come Monday he would have to start all over again. He rushed back downstairs and skidded into the kitchen, to keep an eye on his senile mum, who had thankfully regained her faculties and was already preparing his favourite meal of spaghetti hoops on toast. Finishing his tea, except for one extremely soggy and floppy piece of toast, Josh shouted to his mother with a mouthful of spaghetti hoops: 'See you at five, Mum.' and like a professionally trained circus clown, he picked up the remaining piece of toast with one hand, whilst at the same time scooping up his plastic plate in the other, which he spun across the kitchen with a well rehearsed accuracy into the washing up bowl. Skidding out of the back door he jumped on to his waiting skateboard (like a cowboy jumping on to his horse) and rode it down the garden path towards the gate. When he reached it he jumped off, opened the gate and entered the street where he finished his toast whilst in a rather silly pose that he had adopted against his garden fence, in order to make it seem like he'd been there for some time, and waited for his friends to emerge from their houses. Once they were all out and in equally silly poses, they'd converge on the playground in the middle of the field, on the other side of the road. After half an hour or so of playing the usual game of seeing who can go the highest on the swing – whilst trying not to be knocked off by a football travelling at great speed towards the unlucky one of them on the swing – phase two would come: 'Kerby', on the road near the houses for another thirty minutes or so, until one by one, they would disappear again, until the next day, like drones in a science-fiction film. Josh was screaming inside with boredom, so he said he was going in, and left his friends playing the same old games they'd played every Friday evening for as long as he could remember. On his way back to his house, Josh noticed a piece of notepaper rolled into a ball at the side of the road. He picked it up, sat down on the path and unravelled it, expecting it to be the usual rubbish belonging to one of the girls, like 'so-and-so loves so-and-so', but it wasn't. What it said, in big capital letters, was: WHAT YOU CAN'T SEE, CAN'T HURT YOU. Confused as to why somebody would want to discard such a pearl of wisdom, Josh put it in his pocket and made his way back home. His dad's car was outside the front of the house; surely he would have a good idea of what was meant by the puzzling sentence and a reason as to why it had been discarded in the street. His dad had barely the time to sit down with his cup of coffee, when Josh ran into the lounge and jumped on to the settee next to him. 'What's the emergency, and why have you got your shoes on the settee?' his dad said as he tried to stop his coffee from spilling; Josh complied with the easy part, by kicking his shoes off and halfway across the lounge, just missing Phoenix the cat by an inch. Then came the hard part; the question! He cleared his throat, and mentally pieced together and prepared his question. 'Dad, I found this screwed-up piece of paper outside with writing on it, can you tell me what it means?' he asked, as he handed the piece of paper to his dad. "There's nothing on it," his dad said. Josh snatched the piece of paper back and as he looked at it, he was able to see the last two letters fade and disappear. 'Sorry, Dad, I must have dropped it,' Josh said, putting the piece of paper back in his pocket. 'Can I go back out for a while?' With his shoes already on, and not waiting for an answer, Josh raced out of the front door. Once outside, he fumbled around in his pocket, pulled out the scrap of paper and unscrewed the puzzle. Just as he thought – there, in big bold lettering, was the sentence as before. But as he looked at it, the letters began to jumble themselves up and reassemble themselves, making a whole new phrase that read: WHAT CAN YOU SEE? Puzzled by what it was telling him to do, he looked long and hard at everything around him, but saw nothing out of the ordinary. So he closed his eyes, took a deep breath, let it out slowly, and opened his eyes again. This time, it was different. The first thing he noticed was a procession of ants in a long line that was almost as long as the street. Then he noticed a butterfly dancing to a symphony that was out of a human's hearing range. And then almost as large as life itself, a grasshopper hopped right across the pavement in front of him and hid itself under a rose bush. Josh felt a bit guilty about the fact that all of this life was going on right in front of him, quite literally under his nose, and yet he had never taken the time to notice it before. He put the piece of paper back in his pocket, crossed the road and wandered on to the field, where his friends were still playing that monotonous game. They didn't seem to notice him, which suited Josh just fine, as he sat down on the grass to quieten his mind and to shut out all the noise of his friends, passing cars, mums hollering at their children and the music coming from the bedroom windows of the older kids that lived in the street. One by one, he shut them out, until his thoughts returned to the nice things that nature had placed around him. Reaching into his pocket, he foraged around through the empty crisp bags, chocolate-bar wrappings and general junk, and pulled out the ball of crumpled paper. Uncrumpling it, he held it out in front of him, only to see the letters jumble themselves up again, and come together to read: CAN'T YOU SEE?

Josh closed his eyes and again inhaled deeply, as he prepared himself before opening his eyes once more. This time, the world didn't look at all nice like it had before; instead, it looked dark and forbidding. The branches and the leaves on the trees had turned putrid in colour and seemed starved of nutrients and all the things that it needed to flourish. Looking down at the field beneath his feet, he noticed that the grass was sparse and what had survived had turned a mustard yellow with a greyish border and brown veins running through it. The trees' roots had come to the earth's surface, as though gasping for air, inadvertently killing the small flowers that had found shelter around the trunk, itself in need of a great big dose of sun and rain. No sooner had Josh thought it, than the heavens had opened and poured down a seemingly welcome shower on to the parched earth. It tasted the same as a dead battery might taste; it burned his face and arms and made holes in his jeans, it peeled the paint off the parked cars in the street, whilst the ones that still drove down the road blew black exhaust smoke up at it, almost as a gesture of defiance. The already thick and congested grey air seemed to consume the fumes greedily. There were no butterflies or ants; in fact, there was no sign of life anywhere to be seen, other than the people who were oblivious to the environment that they had created for themselves. Life just carried on regardless. Josh sat down on the roadside and tried to work out why he had been shown these two opposite worlds. He pulled the notepaper out of his pocket again, unravelled it and read: YOU CAN'T SEE! Josh scratched his head. He rolled the paper up and unravelled it again, to see if he could understand the next part of the puzzle. This time, all that was on the paper was the word: EARTH! He was getting more than a little confused and frustrated, so, angrily, he threw the paper down into the road and watched as it unravelled again: WHAT HURT YOU? 'Not having all the answers, so I guess it was ignorance,' Josh mumbled to himself. WHAT CAN'T YOU SEE? 'The consequences of our actions; the future," he replied. WHAT CAN YOU SEE? 'The tangible, as opposed to the intangible.' Where did that come from? Josh wondered. YES! SEE WHAT HURT YOU! SEE WHAT YOU HURT! Josh's face lit up as he realised for the first time that each time that the paper had unravelled itself to reveal a new statement or question for him, it had been made up from the first note he had unravelled: WHAT YOU CAN'T SEE CAN'T HURT YOU. All he had to do now was to work out what it meant. It took Josh many years to even begin to understand the message. He still has the notepaper to this day; but now it's just an empty piece of paper, with no message on it.

This statement has as many connotations as there are stars in the sky. What do you think it means?

Mount Sinai

We all have to go to our own place in the desert,
in order to climb to the top of our own Mount Sinai,
in order to find our own purpose for being.
If and when the realisation becomes apparent,
we can descend the mountain.

Proof

The next time that you ask for proof,

or a sign, or forgiveness; for your lying.

Spare a thought

for the families of the children that are dying.

If youth is wasted on the young,
is wisdom wasted on the old?

What Will It Take

Now in 2007, we are being told that global warming is
melting the ice caps;

and that the greenhouse effect has caused the
temperatures and the oceans to rise.

We are being shown maps of how it will be;

of disappearing islands, and the reshaping of our
continents.

The all-too-late rejuvenation of the rain forests,

new initiatives and a greener way of life,

are being put to the people by our governments.

Nothing is being done, whilst it can be done.

What will it take for us to sit up and listen?

Lost and Found

In order for us to find something again;
first it needs to be lost.
In order for us to find ourselves again;
first we need to be lost.

(Don't hide from the truth, as it has sought you out for a reason.)

A Karmic Debt

Carpathian justice;

dealt with a blow,

with blood on my hands;

you ask, how do I know?

A long time ago,

repaid by today;

it had been accepted by me,

that I'd end up this way.

Only once, then struck off,

by the powers that be.

A universal law;

accepted by me.

A universal law,

with words that only I can see.

A Star for my Children

If I could be a star at night, which star would I like to be?
I would like to be the brightest star,
which at night my children could see.

The first law of 'Nature' is self preservation.
The preservation of nature, is the law of one's self.

Still Waters

A richer history comes from somewhere deep inside, not from a coat of arms on a castle wall.

It's an affiliation to a people, a continent, an island; a people and a nation. The marks of a person's ancestral past can't be seen, because still waters run deep.

Tommy

They may be old and they may be grey,

but once they were Tommy; once they had their day.

They signed up in their thousands, not men but boys,

given rifles and bullets, real ones not toys.

They went overseas to fight others the same,

soon realising it was for real, and not just some kind of a game.

Tommy made his name; because he was well trained,

on the battlefields and in the towns, the Third Reich they tamed.

A new people were born, prouder than ever,

and at home in Old Blighty, they knew they would endeavour.

Tommy would move forward, pushing the enemy back,

never giving an inch, and never giving them slack.

When the war was over, they came home to their families, and their wives,

not forgetting those, who gave their youth, and their lives.

As I Say, Not As I Do

What will be, will be; what has been, has been; you want your children to see what you see, but not to see, what you've seen! To be whoever they want to be, but not to be who you have been!

Spirit of the Light

She sat and watched me, with her cold, glary stare;

a million and one wrinkles, and her long white hair.

I looked away, and then I looked back, but she was no longer there.

She did me no harm, in the time she was here,

she made me feel no dread, and she made me feel no fear.

She was a spirit of the light, and she wanted me to see;

that even in the dead of night, she is always there with me.

A gift so small and insignificant, yet given with love, and from the heart, is the greatest and the most precious gift of all.

Sometimes a place pulls you to its warm and welcoming shore;

and sometimes you feel an urge,

to go through a locked or hidden door.

Don't resist it; let yourself go,

to the place which only you and your 'soul group' know.

'Anger is Fear, turned outwards' (Face the fear; and quell the anger.)

Solitude

(Alone; But Never Lonely)
To sit and ponder, and to enjoy just being.
One of many, not doing, not joining, just seeing.
The ducklings follow; in single file to the water.
Whilst on the field, a mum and dad fly a kite;
with their son and their daughter.
To enjoy so many things,
like the bird as it sings.
Then smile to yourself,
not doing, just being.

The Line in the Dirt

Burnt out cities, filled with the burnt out souls of the people, who wander lost; another victory to the super power, another line in the dirt, not crossed; the soldiers on both sides, they wear a gloomy, grey and deathly cloud, the living dead came home from war, carrying their cross and wearing their shroud.

Evolution

Evolution tells us that: 'Man' began as micro-organisms, that had originated, and evolved, spawning from within the depths of the vast oceans. It is therefore quite feasible, if not ironic, that in time we will return to the vast oceans, as nothing more than micro-organisms. (If science is correct.)

Can a past life regression take you homeward bound?
A spiritual journey to a place never found

The hardest thing to do sometimes is to ask for help. It has got nothing to do with ego or bravado,it is something within us that goes back to our pre-infant school days; and stays with us throughout life. So don't get mad, infuriated, or frustrated, when you see me struggling, to do the simplest task; because I'm learning all over again. Only this time, it's a lot harder, because I am aware of how easy it should be to accomplish. (Please Be Patient With Me)

Per Ardva Ad Astra

Reach for the skies, reach for the stars;
do you really think that they would want us, on either Jupiter, or Mars?
We were given a planet, and in time technology was born;
the scientist the devil, the devil with no horn.
He got rich on the fat of the land,
crushing great parts of it, in his bloodied hand.
For a string of letters that followed his name,
he butchered the Earth, Leaving it bleeding and lame.
Reach for the skies, reach for the stars,
do you really think that they would want us, on Jupiter or Mars?
Why can't we be happy? Why can't we make do?
Like a knight with his sword, we run the world through.
'Per Ardva Ad Astra'; no translation is needed,
we're going nowhere, until the lessons are heeded,

Once a Seed; Now a Flower

As the sun shines through the darkness of night, The leaves unfold like the royal tasters ensuring the safety of their ward. First one; then two; then three, one by one sending a signal to the flower: 'It's safe'. The flower starts to slowly unravel its petals; Its majestic foliage. The colours brightly reveal themselves. To display a pod of seeds; ready for the bee's to feast upon, ensuring the survival of its future, through the replanting of its seed; in a far away field, roadside copse or woodland area. The petals and the leaves catch the wind and wave goodbye.

No is the answer we don't want to hear,
in a rejection of ourselves, we all live in fear.

The honeysuckle never tasted of honey,
the dew-drop never fell,
and a secret wasn't a secret,
without someone, not to tell.

I.D

To find one's identification and to know one's self, is something which I still have trouble with at the age of thirty-eight. It probably had a lot to do with why I joined the Army; the only peer group I've ever belonged to, and probably ever will. Even genetically I have never known acceptance, and have therefore always felt like a runner-up, in this human race. It is something which is taken for granted by so many, who have little or no appreciation of the birth right to 'belong.' Yet within our prejudicial and current political climate, and until the ID of an individual plays no part in whether they should live or die, I'm glad I feel no affiliation, and I'm glad that I never will.

Water

Today I sat and looked at water – a commodity as old as time itself. Every drop has been recycled continuously since the beginning of time. If it could speak, what could we learn from it? The water we drink to quench our thirst, was once the same water that fell from Victoria Falls, crashing to the rocks below; playing its part in the continuous erosion of the planet. That same water tried to hold afloat the Armada, as it was defeated by the British navy. That same water gave life to a thirsty child in a Third World country after being taken from the parched, and infertile land; which it had tried in vain to moisten and provide nourishment to, We have tried to harness the power which it has, but we never will. We consider ourselves to be the masters of this planet, but are we?

Friendship

Whether it's a best friend, a husband, or wife, family member or even a colleague, a true friend is someone who will always be there for you. They are the ones who help you, to get through life. You were brought together from across geographical and political divides, distances, and lifestyles; yet there is more often than not a common ground between you. A friend is a precious person, and even though sometimes, you wish that they would give you some space, you would be very lonely if they did!

The Souls of Trees

I used to believe that trees were twisted and tormented souls, who had, whilst down here, done bad.
I envisioned them as deformed, gnarled, and hideous forms,
rooted in the earth, going nowhere, and grounded for the rest of time; and slowly going mad.
They have been planted in places, where now they've got time to observe and to look;
and given all the time in the world, to reflect; about the wrong path that they took.
They are destined to watch us, for ever-more, and to learn that which is good from bad,
and to also be made aware of the consequences, to the decisions they made; and the choices they'd had.
To be shown; 'The distinction between wrong and right' and the difference between dark and light.

North Africa

The armoured vehicles rolled into the small town 15 miles outside Alexandria (a forward reconnaissance team had already secured and made safe the town in advance), en-route to one of the most carefully planned North African campaigns since liberating Cairo. The men knew that it could be their last chance to reflect upon life, and hopefully to relax, before joining the rest of the armoured convoy for the final assault. There was a noisy silence, or rather, at the very least, an awkward sound of idle chatter amongst the men, barely audible outside of their circles. Nobody knew who would be left within their ranks at the end of the following day. Or how many silent prayers and goodbyes would be sent skywards that night, and the next day, whilst advancing through a barrage of enemy artillery and rifle fire. They sat in small circles beside the tanks sipping tea, which seemed almost like madness, but watching them go through this most British of ceremonies, in their forged battle-family units, was enough to bring a lump to the throat of even the most hardened of men. They looked longingly at photographs of loved ones, in an almost meditative state, filled with fields and meadows, It was their only connection to what awaited them upon returning home; it was, and always would be, the only reason to keep on fighting. The entire afternoon was filled with whispered conversations, and as the bitter cold of night rolled in from across the open expanse of the Sahara Desert, the men prepared to stand down for the evening. This act in itself held no credence out in the desert, because there was no such thing as a stand down, just as there was no lowering of one's guard, not even for one moment. In what must have been only a matter of about five minutes, the town descended into total darkness, and the men tried to settle down for a couple of hours of sleep before it was their turn to stand guard. The following morning the sun rose as quickly as it had set, and with it came the uncomfortable scorching desert heat of the day. The men were already in position for stand-to. You could see in their eyes not fear but alertness, as adrenalin rushed through their veins. They each rolled up their beds and cleaned their rifles, whilst the gun crews on the tanks went through their own check lists. They each had their own silent fears, and if they were to die, even the infantry soldiers would rather take a bullet than have the long, painful death of the tank crew members, who would burn to death slowly, as the thing that had shielded them became a furnace and eventually their coffin. Kitted up and ready for the journey which would write them into the history books that so many would never have the opportunity to read, they moved out of the haven of the small town, and into the desert.

The traveller's heart had never belonged,
his soul was never tied,
that's the way he lived his life,
until the day he died.
He never looked lost,
and he never looked sad,
and he never looked cold,
when the weather turned bad.

7/7
London came to a haunting still,
as the killers lay dead,
along with their kill.
Innocent victims,
on their way to work,
as they did every day;
a minute's silence,
filled with the thoughts,
and the words,
we cannot say.

Wisdom is never left to chance,
as chance is sometimes less than wise.

'Today, I will put my problems into perspective and help to break the
chain.' ('As chain is only as strong as its weakest link.')

My Quest

I talk into the light, and I listen for a voice,

to guide me through this fight, the life I have by choice.

Angel, open your wings, and take me to your heart,

your message it sings, so in life's great scheme,

I will play my part. My angel gives me the strength,
to help me on this quest,

so to all of those that have gone before me,

I promise to do my best.

Uncle Jim

Uncle Jim had lost his legs in an accident, which had happened when the Glider Aircraft that he had been piloting, crashed. I've heard the distinctive sound of his prosthetic steps behind me; on more than one occasion as I was growing up, not at the landmark more important times, but at times when I was being unruly and rebellious. It was as if he had chosen to keep me on the straight and narrow at the times when I found myself at a fork in the road. If I knew that I shouldn't be doing something, but did it anyway, then I would be left to realise the consequences that came with my wrong-doing. If however I had cause to question my own actions; then quite often I would become aware of 'something, or someone, '(my Uncle Jim)', there with me, or I would sense the air around me change, in a way that would make me stop; long enough to usually make me realise; that which I was about to do was on the wrong path in the forked road. I haven't felt his presence for a great many years; not because my every decision is the right one, but because, by now; I 'should' know the difference, between right and wrong.

Teaching

A good teacher is always willing to learn that which is new,
they will listen to another's point of view,
and will welcome change.
They are never too proud to learn from their students.
A teacher is only as good as their 'worst student';
because they are the most testing, and need the most help and
guidance.

Today, I will trust my intuition, and my own inner wisdom.

The Atlanteans

Once there was a city;
so the legends say,
where people's lives were filled with music,
and magic all day.
Nobody knows why,
but one day the city sank,
leaving the place where it had once stood,
empty and blank.
Their spirits lived on
in a non-human form,
into the bodies of dolphins,
they were reborn;
and when it is your time to go
they will show you the way,
to the place filled with music
and magic all day.

Balance

If we want to be 'balanced', and have a fully 'balanced' life, then first we must identify where our short-fallings lie. These may include health, nutrition, study, loyalty, love and one's self; to name a few. 'Imagine yourself as a river': if there is too much water in you, or if you flow too fast, or even if your river bed is too weak to accommodate the flow, then your banks will burst and the water will no longer be contained. It is a combination of things that caused the river to be out of sync. So in order to regain the balance, and to become synchronized in co-existence with it's surrounding environment, each of the factors would need to be addressed in turn, in order to flow again. Just like the river, you need to look at your life, and where you find any imbalances, you must try to put right one area at a time. Start at the foundations and work upwards.

The Written Word

The written word holds no surprise,
but it can make you sit up;
and make you open your eyes.
Fact or fiction,
happy or sad,
enter the writer's world;
whether it's good or whether it's bad.
On a gondola in Venice,
or on an English lake,
the words will dictate,
which direction to take.
If we look hard enough,
we all have a story to tell,
so think about the words you use;
and be sure to tell it well.

Cause and Effect

Like a baby in its crib screaming for its mother, the planet screams out in the only way it can.

Every time it kicks out or turns, the earth's plates separate, move, and come back together again;

changing the very existence of entire land masses in relation to the planet's seas and oceans.

We have to listen for it calling us to it; only we can make things better, and stop the cycle and the downward spiral.

Every action causes a reaction! We need to change our actions, in order to invoke a positive reaction.

Only we can put a stop to our own destruction! (And our imminent demise into oblivion.)

Ocean Waves

The waves broke against the jagged rocks, and the sea enveloped the beach, as the tide brought it further inland, destroying all that lay in its path, including the castles of sand.

'Why?   (Ulterior motives at the expense of others.)

A question that so many mothers and widows have asked; and will ask.

A question asked by soldiers, when asked (told) to carry out questionable or immoral orders.

A question that so many people have sought the answer to (expecting the universe to willingly give the answer to).

When we were given 'free will', we were also given, 'emotion', 'compassion', 'love',

'hate' and 'ignorance'. We were also given 'option'.

In most societies and within most religions, we enjoy the freedom of free speech.

Even though we may find ourselves chastised, or being ostracised for it. We have the right to say no,

and to find the answer to the question: 'why?'

The Dance of Life

Feel the rhythm, as the music enters your space;
it runs through your body, and brings a smile to your face.
Your body moves in the way that it feels;
your hips rotate, as you kick your heels.
Adrenalin rushes through your body, and lactic acids burn,
you hunger the dance, as the movements you yearn.
Addictive properties make you want more,
Endorphins guide you, on to the dance floor.

I Can't See:

where or how it is, that we've come a long way,
The cave dwellers were more civilised than we are; today.

The Men with No Name

A different coloured skin; yet in every way the same,
off the ships from far away; off the ships they came.
Known only by their tribal marks; and by the number
burnt in deep,
all those people that looked on, at night how did they sleep?
The world for them turned to grey; and had become a
different place;
their lives before that day, had been erased without a trace.
Yet within every pair of shackles, and at the end of every
chain,
there was a man; not a number; there was a man who
had a name.

People

Those people who do nothing but annoy us,
are more often than not the people who have been placed in our paths.
They are the ones who we can learn the most from;
whether it's patience, tolerance, compassion or unconditional love.
Identify those people who have been a part of your life, both past and present;
and identify what you learnt from them.

Children of Africa

The drum beats faster, as do their brave hearts.
My ancestors go to war, to defend their freedom, each playing their parts.
Children of Africa, if only they knew,
how their oppressors would defeat them,
and their numbers become few.
They fought for their daughters, their sons and their wives,
but their efforts were in vain against the guns and long knives.
They were defeated, shackled and sent far away,
without even a hope, of seeing their families again some day.
It would be a long time, until their descendants had rights,
it's important we don't forget, about their battles, and their fights,
how they triumphed, and how they won, using their heads, and not the gun.
We have come out on top, and must always remember,
how those children of Africa did never surrender.
There was an odd feeling in the air, he thought, as he opened his eyes and hurriedly stretched his limbs. He went to check on his son, who was watching the goats a short distance away, but when he reached his son, he talked so fast that he ran out of breath and had to catch it again before continuing. The gist of it was that he had experienced the same odd feeling. After settling his son down, he told him to run as fast as he could back to where the rest of tribe had slept the night before, and, without causing any alarm in the women and children, tell the tribesmen to return with him as soon as they could.
Off he ran across the open expanse of the sun-scorched plain,

returning in no time at all with the rest of the tribesmen. After sitting in a large circle for some time, one of the less patient younger men of the tribe got up to return for his morning meal, when a loud bang was heard, which sent the birds in the trees into a frenzy, and the air began to fill with the strange smell of gunpowder. It sent a message of danger to the men, and they set about making a plan. The tribe was one of goat–herders, not warriors, but luckily they were used to defending their herds from wild animals. The tribesmen returned to where their families were, and once there, they nervously armed themselves with spears, drums and shakers, as they said their goodbyes. The tribeswomen wanted to cry and to show their concern, but they didn't – it wasn't their way – they just huddled around the central cooking fire, providing each other with what little comfort they could, as they waited for the men to return. They waited, and waited, but they never did.

All of the riches in the world,
all the jewels, the silver and the gold,
can't replace the loving and tender voice of a parent,
as the lessons they've learnt are told.

Dreaming

With your head on your pillow, you go softly to sleep,
to a most magical place, where your secrets you keep.
You don't need a key to open the box,
you're in the land of no doors and no locks.
It is a most magical place, that is shared by us all,
filled with secret wishes, and the sandman's call.

Are You an Optimist

If the glass in front of you is half full;
then maybe you're an 'optimist',
If it appears half empty;
then maybe you're a 'pessimist',
If you just see a drink;
then maybe you're just 'thirsty'!

All that I own in a pocket or two,
my feet are wet through;
there's a hole in my shoe.
In a pauper's grave I will more than likely end up,
with no one to mourn me,
or to drink from my cup.

Dancing around the camp-fire,
sat on toadstools whilst telling jokes,
no more than an inch in height,
these are the forest's 'little folks'.

Fire

I flicker if the wind blows me,
I turn to liquid as I melt;
even witches were scared of me,
as the licking flames they felt.
The heat becomes unbearable,
keep your loved ones at arms length,
because if you don't extinguish me,
I grow from strength to strength.

SCS St Andrews/Malta

SCS (Service Children's School) St Andrews Malta, at a
young and tender age.

Did I learn much whilst I was there? I really couldn't
gauge.

School just filled the gaps, when I wasn't at the beach.

My mind was not receptive to what my teachers had to
teach.

We didn't have television over there; we would do family
stuff instead.

Our days were always filled with things until it was time
for bed.

There was always somewhere new to go, something to
see or something to do,

an experience, an adventure; a life memory; always new.

They were my years of innocence; and they will always be
with me –

donkey carts on dusty roads, surrounded by the deep
blue sea.

Once bitten, twice shy, three times and you are probably doing
something wrong.

King and Country

The men from the press gang sat in the shadows of the tavern, watching
and waiting for the gullible drunk to accept money for a drink from
them. The next morning, the victim of his own greed awoke with the
worst headache of his life, only partly due to drink, but more from the
motion of the ship and the bruise on the back of his head:

He was not alone, down amongst the stores,

he looked around him, but could see no doors.

Why was the ground moving?

What was that strange smell?

He went to the tavern;

and he woke up in hell.

He turned to another man, with a questioning look,

but he was just as confused,

and his head he shook.

From above a hatch opened,

and then came a voice,

'Climb the rope ladder, men; and no you don't have a choice.'

Five years he spent, in the service of the king;

before he was allowed home again,

to see his kith and his kin.

His liberty lost, for the price of a drink,

'when a stranger is over generous,

take a moment, to think.'

Chain Reaction

We think that our problems are worse than anyone else's, and that the world will come to a grinding halt if they are not put right. The truth is that our problem is no worse than that of the person stood in front of us in a queue. The world is full of people and whole nations, with real problems. If you were to rectify your problem, and the person in front was to rectify theirs, and so on, and so on, then a chain reaction would be formed. And even though the larger world issues may not be solved, the world would be a much happier place to live in; at least for you and the other people in the queue.

Petticoat Lane

It is early in the morning,
the market traders are setting up their stalls.
All kinds of goods are there to be sold,
everyone is equal, the young and the old.
The shouting starts,
the punters are here,
it's a competition to see whose shout is the loudest,
as the morning shoppers get near.
I hope that there will always be,
a Petticoat Lane for our children to see.
Where every one's a 'Darlin' or every one's a 'Luv',
unless you're a gentleman and then you're a 'Guv'.
I'll leave you with this vision just to keep you going,
it's the middle of winter, it's cold and it's snowing.
Mulled wine and cockles; furry hats and gloves.
It's the only place in London,
where these ladies are called 'luvs'.

In order to get the most out of life;
we need to learn to 'keep it simple'.

'The good old days' always seemed better; (but were they?)

'The beggar' does more for 'the giver',
than the giver does for the beggar!

Mexico: (Still a Mayan Kingdom.)

A Dream Fulfilled

To swim with the dolphins had been a dream of his for as long as he could remember. He travelled halfway around the world to Cancun in Mexico; and able–bodied or not, if swimming with the dolphins was at the top of his wish list, that was exactly what he was going to do. All the legends and mystery that surrounded these magical creatures of the sea had always intrigued Patrick; to him, the dolphins were right alongside the legend of King Neptune and his harem of mermaids. As he looked down and saw them, his eyes almost popped out of his head in disbelief. He was bursting at the seams with excitement as he joined them, and he was introduced to Maggie and Odessea. The next hour was filled with a lifetime's worth of emotion as he swam with the dolphins. Their flesh was warm, with an indescribable feel, almost like that of the plump cheeks of a newborn baby, yet taut and muscled, the feel of the dorsal fin as it glided past him almost at one with the clear blue water, which was teeming with brightly coloured angel fish, made him almost cry with elation. He pinched his hand to make sure he wasn't dreaming, he wasn't! In the next moment, he was flying through the air, propelled by these two magnificent creatures, and he bonded with them, in a way that he could only describe as subliminal; 'and not of the here and now!' as they shared their ocean with him. The magic of the Caribbean Ocean had lived up to all of his dreams and expectations; it had been one of the most spiritually and emotionally uplifting experiences of his life. In the envelope of time that was his then, he had only one choice; to surrender his physical body to the universe; his very essence and his soul had achieved a level of consciousness that was only to be felt in this physical lifetime. He felt as though all of his Birthdays and his Christmas's had been rolled into one. That one day in Puerto Aventures, Isla Mujeres, Mexico.

Today, I will look beneath the surface,
of myself and those around me.

The Green Green Grass of Home

(The Grass May Wither and Die; but the Memories Live On.)

Forget about the sunshine and the beaches to roam,

we've got the green green grass of home.

The English countryside is a beautiful sight,

in the heat of the day, and in the cool of the night.

In some areas the ground is so green,

and the grass is the greenest that you've ever seen.

Bordered by paths, which have been there forever,

almost hidden by bushes, Cowslip and Heather.

Across the cattle grid, over the stile and through the gate,

it's time to go home, before it gets late.

Memories of my childhood take me there,

memories of the Cotswolds I would like to share.

Outside it was there, outside the front door,

all that green green grass – who could ask for more?

The Five Tenets of Taekwondo (an ancient warrior code, in a modern context)

- Etiquette
- Modesty
- Perseverance
- Self Control
- Indomitable Spirit

An Explorer's Tale

The Summer is over; Winter is around the corner, and it is definitely Autumn. There are new colours on the ground with a crispness in the air. A very new outdoors, and well worth exploring. Dressed for the arctic weather and with a chocolate bar in my pocket, off I went. The first obstacle was the main road (via the zebra crossing and aided in my mission by the lollipop lady). The first obstacle breached; I was confident that this had to have been my finest hour. I went through the wrought-iron gates and skirmished my way across the open ground, towards the large looming building, where I found myself amongst fellow adventurers. Then the door swung open; almost instinctively, my comrades and I sat down with the grace and agility of a herd of rogue elephants, and then the moment came that I had dreaded all summer (pause): 'Patrick Webber,' came the shout, which reverberated over our heads. There was no going back now; 'Here, sir,' I replied

– and so begins another year in junior school.

For Our Sins

He was not alone up there on the hill;

he had never cursed his captors, and he never wished them ill.

He had time to reflect; whilst he was up there,

he had always shown love, compassion and care.

His mother Mary cried at his feet;

he said, 'Stand up, Mother; evil we shall defeat.

I am up here now, because I'm willing to die for their sins,

but it's after my death, that the real work begins!

So forgive Judas, he regrets very much what he has done,

the battle is over, but the war for Christianity has just begun.'

The symbol of my faith, shall be this cross to which I'm nailed.

A symbol of faith, within us all, of having tried so; never failed.

It's What We're Good At

It's human nature to complain and to moan about everything;
and to consider ourselves hard done by, when we are not;
and to turn a blind eye to those who have a reason to moan, but
seldom do!

Problem Solving

If you have either a problem or an issue that is unresolved, then try
the following: write that which you wish to be rid of on a piece of
paper. With every good intention, read the problem(s) aloud; whilst
you tear the piece of paper up, and put it in the bin. (Although this
is not a technique that has been proven to work, if the intent is there
and if you have exhausted all other avenues, what harm could it
possibly do?)

What Price

(Redemption is earned; and not given freely.)
The seat of power,
or the top of the pyramid,
you cannot split the two;
human sacrifice in any form,
is evil through and through.
The steps to heaven,
aren't stained with blood;
instead they're pure and white.
You will stand beside your enemies,
and walk into the light.

Papa Two One

Zero Alpha, this is Papa Two One, send sit rep over;
(pause)

Zero Alpha, this is Papa Two One, send sit rep over;
(pause)

All stations, this is Papa, Two One over; (pause)

Where is everyone? Why don't they reply?

Please don't leave us out here to die.

Pack up your kit men, and leave all the rest.

Who is reading the map? Who is the best?

Remember what we've been taught; let's work as a team,

If we're to get out of this, I've got to treat the men mean.

Don't worry about your loved ones back home,

they've got you for life, but the army has you on loan.

Where Am I?

I'm not hurting any more!

the last thing I can remember, I was hitting the floor.

I feel nice – enlightened – surely that can't be right!

All of my life I've been bad, I even died in a fight!

Oh good! A library, at least there's something to do,

I know my way around, but it all seems so new.

I can't help feeling that I've been here before,

but I was someone else;

and I came through a different door.

It's all coming back to me now,

I chose my own beginning; just as I chose my own ending.

In a far–off country; whilst strangers defending.

Let me know the results won't you!

I think I'll have a lie down;

for a year or two.

My Desert Rose (Is a life without a love, a life at all?)

I met someone who taught me the true meaning of love;
she taught me about life,
and she taught me about death!
We met on the day that the heavens folded their wings around the
earth; and caused an eclipse of the sun;
in a far off country, that rose up out of the Sahara Desert.
We would sit and talk for hours and hours into the night.
The subject never mattered; it was the company that enlightened me.
I know now that it wasn't just the location,
because all these years later, we can still sit and talk for hours and
hours about life,
and I'm still learning.
I appreciate her as more than just my teacher;
I love her and I always will.
Entwined into each others lives,
she makes my path easier to navigate;
and its storms easier to weather.

The Top Shelf: (To the Victor, the Spoils.)

Everyone that he knew was able to reach up high,
when no one was there; he was going to try.
A cupboard would do, not the stars in the sky.
He positioned his chair underneath, just right;
then lifted himself up using all of his might.
Within his grasp, almost there,
he could feel his hand slipping, and fell back in his chair.
He heard a noise then a movement and it fell,
the jar from the top shelf,
no one would believe him; who could he tell.
He had reached the stars after all;
they had heard his plea; and answered his call.
When he went to bed later that night,
he thanked them for listening, but first making him fight.

Aware

I became truly aware, of all around, whilst standing in a trench, which I had dug in the ground.

With my sights trained on the tree-line, one hundred yards ahead, I noticed all the insects;

with whom I had shared my bed. The morning mist had risen, leaving a crispness and a dew;

I stood there in contradiction to all that nature knew.

What made me open my eyes to all around,

was noticing, how easily it could all be manipulated; to suit our needs,

whilst I stood, in a trench that I had dug in the ground.

Drugs – The Placebo Effect

(Health Is Not Valued until Sickness Comes.)

Doctors and nurses they don't listen to me,

I'm hurting all over, why can't they see?

I'm given drugs to merely mask my pain,

but ten minutes later, the pain comes right back again.

They've all got fancy names, I'm sure; designed to confuse,

but in this long game of life, it's always us that lose.

Green ones, red ones, there are drugs of every hue,

there are so many drugs that I should take, I can't remember what they do.   ·

I'm grateful to our health system as without it I'd be lost,

because in any other country, my care would come at cost.

I'm sure a cure will be found one day; that one day past tomorrow,

I'm better off than some I guess; so I really shouldn't wallow.

Tranquillity

The Path to a Tranquil Life;
Is Through a Life of Virtue!
(So they would have us believe.)

Just Rewards

I wonder who invented the shackle,
and I wonder if they are still wearing theirs!

The Invisible Foe

Time is angers medicine;
today's friend,
yesterday's enemy;
and tomorrows judge!
It devours everything that stands in its path.
It heals all wounds;
but afflicts the week;
and finally waits for no man,
and so withers him and makes him old,
in the Seasons of a year.

Focus

Today, I will focus on,
the letting go of all things;
that no longer serve me,
or anyone else.

What lies beyond the reflection that I see? It's the goodness inside; 'it's
the blueprint of me.'

A Mother's Gift

My Mum would recite Wordsworth, Shelley and Khayyam,
as well as other famous poets,
who have played a part in who I am.
From the great Laureates,
to Grandma's Pussy Cat, and Siegfried Sassoon.
Flanders war-torn and bloody trenches,
to daffodils in bloom.
I think the trick is to try to look beyond the written word,
I've tried to think the poet's thoughts,
and how the poem then occurred.
So thank you, Mum, for the introduction to,
the power of the written word, and all that it can do.

The Unconditional Love of a Daughter

I'll never forget, when I was at my lowest, you put your arms around me; kissed me on my forehead; wiped away my tears; and said, 'It's alright, dad, it doesn't matter.' I miss your wisdom, and I miss your innocence. I wonder what you're doing right now, as I wonder every day. I wish right now you would make me smile, in your unconditional and innocent way.
My morning smile; my star at night; and all that's in-between,
I blinked; our special time was gone? The years I have not seen.
Autumn leaves and Winters snow; the years have passed us by.
A young woman stands beside me, the apple of my eye.

Tragedy

The tragedy of poverty is not knowing the feeling of giving.
The tragedy of wealth is never knowing the feeling of truly heartfelt gratitude.

P's & Q's

The horizon at the end of a summer's day,

the paths as they before you lay: time waits for no man,
or so they say.

Sayings bridged by borders, by oceans and seas;

Ps & Qs, so you'll remember, when you're expected to
say please.

You can't take it with you, and you're a long time dead;

no consolation to the dying, as their last rites are read.

Empty sayings since the dawn of time,

like what's mine is yours, and what's yours is mine.

The Earl of Bute:

(What right have we, to stand and judge?)

It was 1928, and England was between wars; I'm sure that if it had known what was to come, it would maybe have been a little less flamboyant and extravagant. As it was, it was a continuation of social event after social event. Weekends filled with alcohol and poor behaviour, and it was on one such weekend that the following story unfolds. There was a clear distinction between two main social groups, the haves and the have nots, and I'm pleased to say that I fall into the latter category. During the Great War I had been batman to Colonel Stokes, who was a man I would happily have laid my life down for. After the war, he had offered me the same job back in Wales, which I readily accepted, it being a very well paid job, and also because they were few and far between in the years that followed the war. The colonel was a direct descendant of the Earl of Bute, but this lineage did not make him a snob, who treated his staff poorly; it was quite the opposite in fact. He was not a finger clicker or, even worse, a whistler, he knew the names and the families of each and every member of his staff, and he insisted on being addressed as 'Colonel', rather than 'Lord Stokes', as this was not a rank which he had earned with blood, sweat and tears; he would say to me that he was lucky to have been born into a life of wealth and privilege, he had not earned the status of the Earl of Bute, but he had earned the rank and status of Colonel Stokes. The colonel had passed away after battling an infection caused by a rusty bayonet tip, which had snapped off and wedged itself between two of his ribs on a cold, foggy morning, during one particular battle after the whistle had been blown and we had gone over the top. It was a time when we almost, and rather unnervingly, became used to stepping over the bodies of friends, hundreds at a time, in an attempt to make ground and take over another trench, which was more often than not a stone's throw away from the old one; so many lives lost, so our future generations could have a good life, free from tyranny. The funeral had taken place several months previous to the weekend in question, and as such, I had been automatically passed down like a child's toy to the next Earl of Bute. I was a man of thirty-seven years of age, being finger clicked and whistled at by a twenty-year-old public-school educated, immature waste of space of a little boy along with all of his pompous friends. It was only the regular wage that I sent home to my wife Karen and our daughter Coral in Colchester, that prevented me from knocking the 'Earl' or one of his friends out. On that particular weekend, the 'herd', as I called them, due to the way in which they all behaved like animals, had decided that a trip to Pembroke Dock was called for. 'My good fellow', as I was referred to, was to go along also, just in case someone stubbed a toe and needed it to be bandaged, or if, heaven forbid, one of them should pick up their wine glass only to find it empty and temporarily suffer the effects of dehydration. The cars were packed with all the essentials of a weekend away – crates and crates of wine – and although I couldn't swear to it, I think I saw a single loaf of bread. I was squeezed into what little space there was left, for a death-defying two-and-a-half-hour drive to our destination. Driving through the country lanes, and observing all the greenery along the beautiful Pembrokeshire coastline, I couldn't help thinking to myself that the colonel would have loved the area, and I was proud of the small part I played in the preservation of it. I could feel myself welling up, losing myself completely in the moment, but I was soon brought back to a noisy reality of beeping horns and shouting, as a poor farmer transferred his sheep across the lane from one field to another. Embarrassed by the ill-mannered mob, I climbed out of my tiny space and into the lane. Once I had regained my land legs, I walked over to the farmer, who bore all the scars of war and its atrocities in his eyes. I apologised for the lack of respect and bad manners displayed by my aristocratic employer. I presumably bore all the same scars in my eyes, as we gave each other a knowing look and a nod, and instinctively knew that we would give our lives for each other. I turned back towards the cars and gave the Hooray Henrys the glare of a lion protecting its pride, and the horns and shouting came to a halt. I turned back towards the farmer and we again shared that knowing look of respect, before he continued on his way into the field. I felt envious of him, as he had not carried on in servitude to another, but instead, he had become the shepherd; unlike me, who seemed destined to live out my life as just one of the herd. Just another sheep! I was more than a slave, and I couldn't help but think for the rest of the journey that I was not living my worth as a human being. The colonel and I held that selfsame respect for each other that had been lost on this generation, and as such, I made a decision there and then that this would be my very last weekend in slavery. I resolved to return to face the man, who had become the shepherd, only this time it would be as a free man, and not as a sheep; the respect of the shepherd meant more to me than all of the lords and ladies in Britain, and I was going to earn it. We drove for five more minutes, until the cars all stopped at the bottom of the hill to Pembroke Castle – a monument to our country's fortitude, and a symbol of its pride. The herd ran up the hill towards the castle's keep under the watchful eye of those who had passed defending it, as the spirits looked down over the battlement; I felt sure that they must have shaken their heads in disbelief, as I often do. I gathered the hampers and the ground blankets together and noticed for the first time that the young Earl hadn't run up the hill with the others – he was standing just a short distance away, looking out to sea. 'Are you ok, sir?' I enquired. 'What's your Christian name?' he replied. More than a little taken aback, I answered, 'Patrick, sir.' 'Mine is Ronald, and I insist that you address me as such until I have earned the right to be called sir.' He extended his hand for me to shake, and in that moment, I could see his father in his eyes. 'Would you mind telling me about my father, the Colonel Stokes that you knew, Patrick?' he continued. 'Nothing would give me greater pleasure, sir – sorry, Ronald,' I replied. 'Don't worry about that lot up there, they won't even know we're missing. In cultures all over the world they would be desecrating ancient burial ground, and would be punished for doing so.' We walked for quite some time, and then sat for a while on the rocks, just looking out to sea. 'If you don't mind me asking,' I said, 'why, after all this time, even going back to when your father was alive, are you enquiring as to who the real colonel was? Surely you could have asked him those questions. He would have been more than happy to relay his stories to you. He would often say to me that he could see himself in you, and he wished that you would drop the facade of the young, country gent, and for you to just be yourself.' 'It's a regret that I will carry with me for the rest of my life, Patrick.' With that, we stood up and wandered on to the rocks. There was a definite difference in him, as though a heavy weight had been lifted from his shoulders. 'I saw the invisible cord between you and the sheep farmer, a brotherhood between old soldiers, the same as that which could not be broken between you and my father. A cord I will never know.' 'Hey! Less of the old!' I said, trying to make light of our conversation. 'What's that over there?' he shouted, pointing out to sea. It was a fishing trawler, and it was on fire. And then the oddest thing happened; it was as though Ronald had become another person, and had morphed himself into his father. Taking full control of what most people would refer to as a situation beyond their control, he ran up the track and pulled his father's army-issue trench whistle out of his jacket pocket. Facing towards the castle, he blew three short sharp blasts on the whistle. To any war veteran within earshot, it was a call to arms, and it had the desired effect, as a string of men who had left their fields appeared from over the brow of the hill. I was quite unprepared for the next thing that happened – Ronald's friends raced down the track, making the amount of potential firemen up to a good score strong. As though it was a rehearsed contingency plan being put into practice, the locals and the group of Hooray Henrys (and that is the last time that I will refer to them as such) launched themselves to the rescue. Three rowing boats were put to the sea, each with an empty boat in which to tow the crew back to shore. An extra boat was filled with empty shrimper's buckets and was tethered to the forward rowing boat, captained by the young Earl. Those left ashore, including myself, ran towards the small hamlet and commandeered as many towels and blankets as possible and returned to the pontoon, in time to receive the first of the evacuees as they came to shore. A crew of twenty-eight were brought safely ashore that day and the damage to the boats was minimised considerably by those in the remaining boats, and a chain of buckets. Ronald and his friends came ashore when the fire was under control. I retrieved a dry blanket and walked over to Ronald. Handing it to him, I said, 'For you, sir,' and it was all I could do to stop myself from saluting him.

Head On

Today, I shall have the courage to face my fears.

Climb Down

If you put yourself on a pedestal,
then be prepared to be knocked off;
(because it will happen).

The early bird catches the worm - but the early huntsman catches the
bird!

Timelines

If the past made us who we once were,
and the future will make us who we can be;
then who are we today?

Informed Opinion

It's only when we let go of our judgements, and the opinions,
which are founded on the truths and preachings of others;
that we are able to find our own truth, and form our own opinions.

Bloodlines:

(more than just geography, that ties me to a place)
I know where the island of Trinidad can be found
a place I've never been, but by bloodlines I'm bound.
The Caribbean Ocean: a place full of dreams,
the more I try to close the gap, the further away it seems.
Plantations full of exotic fruits, and people full of smiles.
A turquoise ocean: bordered by palm trees and golden sands, that
stretch for miles.
I may never get there, but it doesn't mean;
that even in my deepest sleep; I'm not allowed to dream.
I've always wanted to see the towns of San Fernando, Paulo Seco and
the capital Port of Spain,
the places where my Dad grew up, the places that gave me my name.
I'd stand where my Grandpa stood, and feel him in the earth.
I'd be drawn to the places where my family had lived, long before my
birth.
To sit and watch the sun set, and the sky turn crimson red, as it turns
black, my dream is ended, and I'd wake up in my bed.

The Cycle of Life

Ask yourself, any question,

and you may ask yourself why;

its only to make a point, I think,

like why are we born to die?

Family life

The two boys and their little sister put on their anoraks and wellies; well,
the boys managed, but their sister was hopping up and down the
hallway with one boot only half on. After another good ten minutes of
sorting herself out, they were ready for the off. Their mum and dad had
been spying on them, and, judging by their faces, had been laughing at
their antics in getting ready. 'Have you all got your gloves?' their mum

asked. It was pretty hard not to, thought the younger of the two boys to himself, as he pulled his gloves from his pockets and tugged on the embarrassing piece of string that joined them together around his back. His sister giggled in that annoying little sister way. 'Right, ready at last,' said their dad, as he reached for the door keys. All the way up their street, the three children tore off happily in front. 'Stop messing about near the road and save your energy for when you get to the woods,' their dad shouted. On the way there, they passed a small shop, and their dad went inside to buy a large bag of bonbons. He gave them all one bonbon each with a dual purpose in mind: the first was to keep them quiet, and the second was as an incentive to behave themselves. Quietly, they continued on their way, with their little sister holding her dad's hand and the boys walking together taking in the many sights and sounds. 'Look, Mum, there's Tufty!' the younger of the two boys exclaimed; he would always call squirrels Tufty, like the character in one his favourite television programmes. It was only a short walk to Bluebell Woods, but it was always filled with sound teachings by their mum and dad about the world that resided at the end of the street.

The Cobbled Path

Leaving it all behind you, leaving the life you know;
you step on to the cobbled path, but you don't know which way to go.
You look back towards your family, hoping they'll tell you which path to take,
but this journey is about you; it's a decision that only you can make.
No coin to toss, no straw to pick, you look up to the sky;
disheartened at the lack of help, you sit on the kerb, and sigh.
The path you take is not the challenge, you must realise you're not alone;
as you walk along the cobbled path, you'll reap the seeds you've sown.
The journey seems long and lonely, although along the way,
you will meet all kinds of people; listen to what they say.
Although the path is sometimes hard, and sometimes you feel weak;
carry on regardless, if it's answers to your questions that you seek.
When you meet a fellow traveller, who can answer what it is that you ask;
you can at last go home,
and take off your earthly mask.

Balancing Life, with Death

Life, live, living, lived,
death, die, dying, died;
the fragile balance which is.

Demons & Dragons

You cast your own shadow, like you build your own wall.
You choose whether to go down, the alley with no door.
Freedom of choice lets us decide,
whether or not we go to the place, where our demons
reside.
If you face your fears, and defeat what lies deep,
you will lay 'your' demons and dragons to sleep.
Face your demons, when they present themselves to you;
listen to your soul and you will know what to do.

At Her Majesty's Pleasure

The sun is rising;
I had better sit on the floor,
facing the bars,
with my back against the door.
When the sun shines through the bars,
and casts shadows across the floor,
I reconnect with life;
the life that I had before.
As long as I have my shadows,
I will have that appointment to keep;
a reason to get up in the morning;
and a reason at night to sleep.

The Oath: (Blood-oath)

The Oath of Allegiance,
is like a handshake,
you make a promise;
a promise you can't break.
It's all well and good
standing proud and tall;
but there's no room for pride,
as your mates around you fall.
They never showed you videos,
or told you how you would feel,
when the Queen called you to arms,
and how your heart wouldn't heal.
A civilian will never know friends like you had;
friends who were always there,
through the good times and the bad.
They would take a bullet,
rather than see you hurt;
your brother in arms
hits the dirt.
His last words muffled,
by all the commotion; in your head,
you remember the Oath, and the words you said.
The Oath you took,
and by it you're bound;
forever in your dreams,
your friend's last sound.

A Night at the Proms: (Blinkered)

Balmy summer, now there's a phrase;
it's how we the English, describe hot sunny days.
We wait hours in the rain,
to wave paper flags at the Queen;
to remember the elegance, and the 'majesty seen'.
Ladies curtsey and gentlemen bow,
who thought of that?
What's wrong with an acknowledgement,
like a tip of the hat?
Strawberries and cream,
watching them sweat;
stand up and cheer,
when the ball goes over the net.
Don't get me started
about our parliament and the law;
or about that house in London,
with number ten on the door.
We are a nation full of hypocrites,
cast out from the rest;
on this tiny island,
that only we think is the best.
Open your eyes and see all that is out there;
see the whole picture, and take a moment to care.
Then go back to your 'balmy summer,'
now there's a phrase,
it's how we the English describe,
hot sunny days.

Spring Time

Spring time so fresh,
as the new lambs are born,
the Summer's sun sets
and the fields are full of corn.
Autumn leaves fall,
the scenery so nice,
the frosty Winter morning calls,
bringing the cold, and the ice.

Your Painting

I ask you, the Reader,
to close your eyes, not tight,
and let your mind drift,
as though it were night.
In your mind's eye you see a canvas,
and paints of every hue;
sit down at your easel, and I'll tell you what to do.
With your eyes still gently closed, look at the view,
then turn to your canvas –
crisp, white and new.
Remember; any work of art is judged by each and
everyone;
but this one is exclusive –
it's yours when it's done.
Let the colours flow, and let the subject be transformed,
your painting, like your life, not falsely adorned.
A period, an age, a phase of time;
conveyed by the brush,
a mere shape, a mere line.
The painting never finished goes on and on,
for others to interpret;
'but not until you're gone'.

Who Was It?

Who was it who said 'live your dream'?
I've spent all my life trying,
but what does it mean?
I've tried till I dropped,
till my hands and feet were red-raw,
I've climbed mountains, and looked down,
to see what he saw.
I've travelled far and wide,
I can't travel any more;
everywhere that I've been,
leads to another shut door.
It's only now that I've stopped looking,
that I can really see;
what is meant by 'live your dream',
and be all that you can be.
My dreams have changed;
I've grown into my skin;
I'm pleased to report,
nearly four decades in.

The 'Hypocrite' (the Hippocratic oath)

The reason for someone's entire life scheme or path could be altered by being saved from a preordained exit point. Has anybody been given the universal right to change the equilibrium that is the way of this world (and this universe)? Yet it would be considered to be inhumane to stand idly by and do nothing, whilst watching the suffering of another person.

It doesn't matter whether we are rich or poor, young or old;
every wrong that we do, comes back 'tenfold'.

The Law

The law; can and does,
protect us
from everything,
except itself;
its clauses,
and its by-laws.

Inspiration: (in spirit nation)

I ask of spirit to shower me in light,
so that I can share with others,
a most glorious sight.
A sight of valleys, of mountains,
and summer-fresh fields.
Filled with new spirits,
revelling in the crops that it yields.
At the beginning of their journey,
many levels to go,
I look behind me at the field,
now covered in snow;
bare feet walk through it,
not cold but warm,
like the dew that follows night,
in the new light of dawn.

Live it;
and if attainable,
then be it;
don't just dream it!
(Having never even tried it.)

55

Serendipity

If only we knew, how our lives would all work out.
If only we knew, what it was all about.
Faces from our past, modelled out of clay;
were those faces that we were destined, to meet some day.
A snapshot of time, that never meant much,
were those moments in time, that our souls would touch.
Serendipitous lives, going about their days,
living their lives, in serendipitous ways.

Into the Valley

A tale of courage, a tale of dare;
a tale is but a tale,
unless you were there.
Into the valley of death,
never to come out;
all of those sons and daughters;
their fathers without.
From a tale of courage,
to a tale of woe;
as those fathers on horseback,
into the valley they go.
A chapter, a period, a deed in time,
they entered the valley, the horses in line.
In our history books
they will always remain,
those brave soldiers on horseback;
the six hundred fathers with no name.

Today; I will appreciate
each and every person in my life
who I would miss if not here.

The Travelling Showman

Take your seats please, ladies and gentlemen,
the show's about to start.
It's my duty to warn you first,
it's a tale that will break your heart,
first we'll go to the place,
where God gave us his son,
divided by the Gaza Strip,
and where every child has a gun.
Then heading south,
where the stories are much the same,
people hunting people, people hunting game.
Can you guess how it ends,
or do you need to see more?
It is much the same all around the globe,
of that you can be sure.
The show is finished, folks,
which is a statement in itself;
are we just repeating history?
Are we just a show on a shelf?

Trapped

Try to avoid becoming trapped by a title;
so you won't miss it when it is taken from you!

The ocean's depths, and golden sands,
made with love, by our creator's fair hands.

Yin & Yang

False Prophets,
Wizards,
Shaman and Seers,
throughout history,
have been victimised,
by superstition, and fears.
Stone circles, Druids,
and ancient beliefs,
from the Rosetta Stone,
to the Egyptian reliefs.
Mankind has gone full circle,
and it's from ourselves we learn;
the ancient ways were tried and tested,
and it's to those ways we turn.
People who were gifted,
made others question being,
so in ignorance they lived their lives;
in denial, never seeing.
To every coin there's a flip side,
to every yang a yin,
those who used their gift for good;
and those who hungered sin.
The witches burnt in village squares,
they died to pave the way,
for all the many healers,
who practise here today.

Value what you feel is important in life;
without putting a value, or a price tag on it.

The Natural Order of Things

People kill people! Ignorance kills people! Fear and prejudice kill people! Insecurity kills people!

Poverty kills people! Jealousy and envy kill people! Environment kills people!

From the moment that we are born, the battle begins;

and the endless fight for survival, is set in motion.

A learned person, can spell the word 'modest', but they choose not to;
(at least not publicly!)

The End of the Day

As the sun goes down
on another day,
we give thanks for a society,
that lets us have our say.
We go through our lives,
with our own free will,
a life full of choices; and yet still.
Sometimes the wrong path,
looks like the better choice.
Sometimes we've got things to say,
but we can't find our voice.
So when you have your chats
with those who lend an ear,
say thank you for your lives,
give thanks for being here.
Say thank you for the choice to choose,
whether to be on the side that wins;
or whether we choose the choice to lose!

Fly Free

You owe it to yourself,
to be as free a spirit as you can possibly be,
and to fly through a sky that knows no bounds.

The Indian Princess

To circumnavigate around the world,

I thought was its own reward.

You can imagine how pleased I was, upon leaving one port,

when an Indian princess was brought on board.

In China we were given lengths of royal silk or
sometimes tea,

but this payment of rarest of jewels,

I was sure would incite mutiny.

I entered into the captain's log;

that we had on board,

a cargo that would be,

more deserving of a lord.

By rights she was goods,

to barter with, exchange or sell,

but if I was to let that happen,

then surely I would go straight to hell!

I looked through my telescope,

and saw the Sultan in tears,

with his head in his hands, as he realised his fears.

When he saw our return, he ran out into the water;

all the spice in India, could not replace the Sultan's
daughter.

Hourly Bulletins (sleeping with the enemy)

7.00 p.m., 8.00, 9.00 then 10.00, the news tells us stories,
about men killing men.

Pictures sent by satellite or via picture phone,

of all that's bad in the world, beamed right into your
home.

Pictures of war, natural disasters, famine and crime;

who's killing who, who's homeless, who's starving, and
who is doing time.

You go to sleep, with pictures planted in your head;

they've done their job well, the medias in your bed.

Bluebell Woods

Whittling wood, and learning
how to leave and follow broken twigs,
we would learn the ways of the woodsman,
even though we were only kids.
When I see a patch of bluebells now,
I'm transported to those woods in the spring,
'and even now', although I'm all grown up,
I still smile at the memories they bring.

Someday I'll write a story,
about all the weird stuff that goes on in my head,
and how all the really odd stuff up there,
I usually save,
for when I'm tucked up in bed.

Wasting

I'm wasting away,
every day I can do less.
I get confused about the words I say,
all because I've got MS.
Those people that look on,
do they really understand.
What it is, to break your fall,
when you can't find your hand.

Watching

Faces on the school buses, as they drive by,

in the prams, hidden faces, all that you hear is a cry.

On every high street; in every shop; at every turn.

Take notice of it all, turn it around, be analytical, what
can you learn?

Look at the lines on their faces, both the young and
the old,

What do they say to you? What secrets do they hold?

Some walk fast, whilst others walk slow,

as if without purpose, with nowhere to go.

The emotions are there, for all to see,

happy, sad, pensive, or reflective like me.

I wonder which of them is thinking my thoughts;

and I wonder what they think of me?

Looking at the lines on my face, seeing; what I cannot see.

Realise your dreams,
no matter how small;
so that you'll have no regrets,
when the other realm call.

A Magical Kingdom

There is a place just the other side of town, where the fairy king governs his population. Highwoods – is the name we give it, but to them, it is the entire universe! If you're very still, and have the patience of a saint, they'll sense that you're not a threat to them, and they will carry on their day as though you were never there. One team gathers twigs to thatch their roofs, whilst another scours the floor at the base of a tree for fallen seeds. A third team appears, and suddenly you feel humbled to be privileged enough to bear witness to this spectacle. A bearded fairy elegantly flutters his wings and floats up on to a tree branch, whilst his entourage sits on the floor and listens to his every word; maybe he's a storyteller passing on what he once heard a storyteller pass on to him. Or perhaps he is a teacher of magic, passing on his secrets to a chosen few. Then almost as quickly as I saw them all appear, they all disappear again, into the undergrowth. I get up and walk away, unsure if I had fallen asleep and dreamed the whole thing whilst I had sat under the tree in the midday sun. So I looked back, and saw what looked like a fairy, stooping down to retrieve a small basket full of seeds. Maybe I hadn't dreamt it after all.

Tick-tock

Tick-tock, tick-tock,
from the humble pocket watch;
to the town hall clock.
Husbands rushing home from their places of work;
children strolling home from their schools;
our world that we've created would be lost,
without all of our schedules, timetables and rules.
Even our histories, are a measurement of time,
Of how the Moon rotates around the Earth, and the stars
fall into line.
The daily rotation of the sun, as your alarm clock rings,
the cockerel crows, and the morning bird sings.

Windows to the Soul

They are such a complex and intricate organ,

and yet they have the simplest name.

The eye or I is always on display,

yet never feels our shame.

They can be used to flirt,

or to influence right from wrong,

to say a thousand words,

or to sing the most beautiful song.

Love, Hate, Sorrow, Contempt, to name but a few,

the messages and images interpreted, and learnt from;
and the messages they can see right through.

It takes an accomplished liar, to control their pupil's
dilation and size,

it's as though they have closed their windows to the soul,

and choose to go through life, wearing a transparent
disguise.

If you look inot somebody's eyes, their pupils will dilate,
shrink or grow,

and the vortex that is the iris opens up, circled by a
celestial glow.

They will reveal a kaleidoscope full of voids,

that come in all shapes and sizes,

it's through these voids that you get a glimpse of the real
person,

a glimpse of their soul, without the disguises.

Times of Old

'The pen (or the quill)
is mightier than the sword',
a scholar once wrote.

Fatherhood

I've learnt the hard way
that which I now know;
a father's job is to be there,
and to help their children to grow!

A Quiet Life

Normality is something that we don't decide,
abnormal we sometimes do,
afraid of what is deemed different,
and distant from anything new.

Resonation

A deep-down vibration,
that I'm unable to feel,
and I'm unable to see.
It's a cosmic vibration,
shared by no one but me.
A vibration that's made,
by movement and breath.
A vibration that's mine;
from my birth till my death

When you are angry count to ten;
when you are hungry count to one hundred.

Pooh Sticks

We've all heard the stories,
of Piglet, Tigger and Pooh.
With my hand on my heart,
I tell you they're true.
I was playing in the woods, on my own one day,
when he beckoned with his paw and said, 'Come this way.'
Following Piglet and Pooh, I stepped up to the mark.
The whistle was blown, provided by the lark.
The sticks afloat, like small canoes in a race,
I was hoping mine was losing well,
or at least had kept good pace.
I dashed to the other side, and looked over;
I'd won!
I'd done what I thought, could never be done.
With my hands triumphantly raised, I turned around to see;
no one;
just one lonely blackbird, high up in a tree.
It never mattered to me, that no one was there;
the day that I defeated, Pooh the bear.

Promises of Peace

'World Peace, Peace in our Time, the Struggle for Peace':
empty, hollow words;
declarations, political agendas and forums,
that fit nicely into an otherwise flat and empty speech;
full of flat and empty promises; never to be upheld.

The Road Home

I woke up, having dreamt that my life, that was my reality, had been a bad dream. I was living in a dream home, with all my creature comforts around me, that everyone takes for granted, but my reality was a very different story. I was homeless, squatting in a squalid, derelict building in a town called Saint-Moritz in France, no more than one hundred miles from the port of Calais – which could be reached easily enough – but I would still need the money to purchase a ticket, for the short ferry ride across the Channel back to England. I had managed to save a meagre eleven francs and fifty centimes, which was hidden behind a loose brick in the wall of the squat. I was fortunate enough to have been befriended by and taken in by two lads of about my age of twenty-one. Names were not generally used, but I think their names were Michelle and Paul, or Jean-Paul. There was no language barrier to break through, as most communication took the form of a language consisting of grunts, groans, pointing and other hand gestures, which were of a universal language. The begging though was in a language that left a bitter taste in my mouth, which could only be got rid of by the vinegary taste of the cheapest cooking wine, which was used quite often as a substitute for an evening meal, as it was cheaper. There was never idle talking as such, or a communal reflection on our days, or the next day's agenda; not even the laughter brought about by our intoxication. There was just the end to yet another day in an existence which seemed as though it would last forever. My bed was the cold, hard floor and my blanket was a mixture of towels, sheets and what must have once been a dog's blanket – tied together in an attempt to afford me a little comfort through the nights – all of which had outlived their usefulness and had been dumped in the skip outside the rear exit door of the supermarché. The row of shops in the precinct was where the majority of my food came from; there was an interlude of five or so minutes, in between the delivery van leaving a number of crates consisting of bread, croissants and cakes, and the arrival of the staff. The trick was to not be greedy and to only take a croissant or two, and maybe a cake for lunch. If I timed it wrongly, I would be shooed away and cursed at like a stray animal. Having eaten, I went to the train station to be a social annoyance to the commuters. The gendarmes were more efficient than I had ever been witness to in England; so I kept an eye on the roads, and if I saw them I would quickly move on. 'Pourriez-vous épargner un peu d'argent pour la nourriture (Could you spare a little money for food?), s'il vous plaît?'

All day, every day, in the rain and the cold, with my feet wrapped in carrier bags to maintain body heat, which would still get so cold some days that I would be unable to feel them as I walked back to the cold and damp squat; my pathetic day's bounty of small change, which had trebled in amount, was usually spent on a packet of cigarettes, which were a good source of heat; and a bottle of cooking wine, which was helpful in getting us to sleep. Warmth would only come from imagining it, in an already overstretched imagination. There is no line of psychology or school of thought that can prepare somebody for a life of such destitution and degradation. No fires were lit and huddled around, because somebody (quite within their rights) might see it and phone the gendarmes. The days were as long as they were short, and as short as they were long, an existence of non-existence, a being of not being. One step forward was followed by two steps backwards. There was no line drawn between day and night – they all mingled into one, as did the weeks. The stench stopped being a stench, the filth wasn't filthy anymore; the damp up the walls that filled my air and saturated my lungs, became normal. The lack of food was only indicated by an occasional loud rumbling sound made by my stomach (after a couple of weeks even my stomach fell silent, with no protest left in it). The cup of icy-cold water, which was used to wash my face, wasn't cold any more – neither was it warm – it just was. That was what I had become – a somebody, but a nobody. One of many soulless shadows, which so many will walk past choosing never to look beyond the outstretched hand. I don't want to go back there in this lifetime,

Yet I am forever indebted to France for teaching me compassion and empathy, but most of all for teaching me humility.

Society

The society in which we live, dictates so much;
the time we sleep and hours spent awake,
which side of the road we travel down,
the rules we live by, and the tests that we take.
The decisions we think are our own, are, in fact,
the decisions that we were destined and expected to make.

The Amphitheatre

Life is a series of plays,
performed in an auditorium to a crowd;
some of which are full of praise,
whilst others find nothing but fault.
You can choose to comply,
and to read from the script;
or, you can write your very own play!

Old Friends

You go by so many names,
which one of them is right?
Where is it that you go?
When day takes place of night!
God willing we shall meet one day,
upon a golden sky,
the ferryman will take me home;
one day when I die.

Through Childlike Eyes

No judgement,
no reason to hurt or lie,
watching rainbows and clouds,
high up in the sky.
It all seems so easy
and so crystal clear,
with no reason to worry,
and no need for fear.

Reality

Somebody made me realise today;
that in our artificial and pre-
fabricated world,
we need to find our own reality.
If we look too hard, we will never
find it,
even though it was there all along,
staring us in the face.
The realisation is the easy part,
doing something about it though,
is going to take the real courage,
which is getting harder and
harder to find;
as the years drift on by.

To my Granny I do often talk, and I hope that she can hear, words not
spoke aloud, though loud enough for my Granny so dear.

Gone! (as though they never were)

The memories I have of living in Germany;

I'm glad they are just memories, of a lifetime ago, of a lifetime in the past.

Cold winters; with adulthood thrown upon me –

times and things that I will never forget, memories that would always last.

A child should never see, the kind of things I saw,

never mind do the things I did; things outside the law.

The system let me down,

I felt dirty, vulnerable and easy;

the world outside my home,

had become sordid, cold and sleazy.

'An adult is an adult'

and should act accordingly!

Out of all the kids in the world,

why did they have to pick me?

To protect and to serve,

a society driven by the law;

no child should ever see,

the things as a child I saw.

I can't put into words, how they stole from me,

the me I took for granted; 'the me the world could see!'

My innocence was lost; I felt emptiness inside,

the part of me that shone so bright, was the part of me that died.

Compromises

Blood was spilt, tears were cried,

and bodies were put into the ground;

another day in our stubborn history,

another compromise not found.

Have confidence in your own abilities,
even 'if ' or 'when' others question it.

Father to Son

When my son was born, it was deep into the night, and I must have smiled until it was light.

I'd never before been part of one of nature's greatest gifts, and when I'm feeling low now, the memory it lifts.

I've seen him grow, into the young man he is today, but I was never there, when he needed or wanted his dad, I regret to say.

He's never asked me for fatherly advice, or asked me about life, what's bad and what's nice.

I hope he has a life full of smiles, just like I like I had on that night, without the need to struggle, and without the need to fight.

One day he'll come to me, and side by side we'll stand;

we'll look into each other's eyes, and I'll offer him my hand.

Like on the night when he was born, he will take my hand to hold, and he'd know how much I loved him, in a language never told.

My Dad

All of my life, I've wanted to be like my Dad;

all of my life, I've wanted the respect that he had.

I would like to thank my Granny and my Grandpa, for giving me my Dad.

I've felt the way that I feel, ever since I was a lad.

Then I grew up, and I became a Dad.

I'm not afraid of my feelings,

and I'm not afraid to say,

'I loved my dad when I was young, but I love him more today!'

Only a Thought Away

They were only small, and full of life, when I met them both, for the first time;

I would like to think that I touched their hearts, as the two of them touched mine.

They never questioned me, and they never said I had no right,

or threw it back in my face, in the ensuing verbal fight.

They had their moments, and so did I, if we fell out though,

I would always be there, when they needed a hug or a cry.

I never refer to them as my Stepsons; I hope that they'll always call me 'Dad',

and remember, just as I do; the many happy years together we had.

Reaching

The art to living,

is knowing your limitations,

and reaching beyond them.

The Mime
To observe the academic at work,
and then to mimic,
with precise accuracy;
surely that is the true genius.

Comfort

Some find comfort from 'within',
whilst others find it from
within a 'religion' or a 'group'.
However we find the comfort
from knowing,
we must never be too busy
to help somebody
who is still searching.

In Memoriam: of Ron

The armies came;

to take our land and to take our
lives,

they rode on horses just as we did,
only they carried rifles, not
knives.

They came from far away and
defaced our ancestral land,

the plains, once full of life,

stood empty, lifeless and bland.

Our once proud people,

were forced to live on a reservation;

we had lost our very essence,

the essence of our Indian nation.

The Scribe: 'He Who Writes'

The scribe had lost his very identity, the family name had been forgotten and first names were only used by the family. Yousef was his name, and this is his story:

Yousef was the scribe to the court of the Pharaoh, and, as such, was a good way up the proverbial ladder of hierarchy. He was answerable only to the higher ranking members of the Pharaoh's army, and any member of the priesthood. It was his job to document anything and everything; it was the Pharaoh's wish that his name, his victories in battle, the monuments and the statues and the temples that had been built in his reign, should live on forever. The day began pretty much as any other. With the sun yet to rise, Yousef sat up on his blanket, which he proceeded to roll up and put to one side, as there was very little space in the home that he shared with three generations of his family. After saying his morning prayers, he put his sandals on and went through to the main area, where the morning's food had been prepared some hours before he had awoken. Yousef broke off a piece of bread, dipped it in a pot of honey and picked up an apple to eat later in the day. Sitting on the floor again, he gave thanks for the provision of the food for him and his family. When he had finished, he picked up his tool bag, which consisted of several rolls of papyrus, a stone tablet, a collection of reeds, which had been cut to a point, and two small pots of ink – one black and the other red – and left through the blanket, which served as a door, and wandered out into the street, where the market traders were already setting up their stalls, consisting mainly of spices, cottons and a range of pottery and earthenware for use in the homes. He arrived at the temple nice and early, and he sat there in the morning sun, watching the world go by, as he did every day, whilst waiting for the Pharaoh and his entourage of architects, priests, officials and generals. The days usually involved his following the procession, who were appointed the task of carrying out the young king's wishes. On that day, however, he was approached by a very short, round man, who had obviously been exerting himself, as his face was bright red and extremely flushed.

Wiping the sweat from his brow and catching his breath, he explained that he had been sent to relieve him of his daily tasks, as the Pharaoh had been taken ill the previous night and would be resting for the rest of that day. Yousef sat back down on the temple steps, tapping his fingers and whistling, whilst thinking how best to spend the day. After a few minutes of contemplation under the scorching sun, he picked up his leather bag and set off for the mountain range some way off in the distance. Yousef was going to regain his identity and find himself again! He had made a point of filling his water flask before setting off, but, still some distance from his destination, he had drunk nearly all of it. For some reason, the mountains seemed the same distance away as when he had left the city's temple steps. One or two hours had passed, maybe three or four, he couldn't tell, and he didn't have a single drop of water left, and the mountains weren't getting any closer. Every time that he looked back at the city, it had gradually disappeared into the distance; even the horizon, it seemed, had drifted away and vanished. He was getting more and more confused, and more and more frightened. He knew the desert and its dangers as well as any of his friends, but this time was different – the lie of the land had changed. Normally, it was possible to map the journey using the sun's position in relation to landmarks both natural and man-made. Nothing was where it should be; it was as though the desert was a carpet that had been taken by two corners and shaken, and when it settled, nothing was as it had been before. Knowing that he had to keep going, Yousef tried to regain his orientation as best as he was able and remapped his new landscape. He had once heard a priest address a small gathering outside the city's walls and recalled the priest having said, 'Set yourself a goal; if it is worth reaching, then along the way you will have to change your direction as many times as is necessary, avoiding any pitfalls along the way. Don't live your life being afraid of making that journey, and never expect someone else to make it for you.' With this in mind, Yousef continued along the new path. After a short while, he stopped and looked around him. He was lost. Then his thoughts returned once again to the small gathering, and he remembered another piece of the travelling priest's sermon: 'If you lose your way through a labyrinth of caves, close your eyes, and like a blind man would, you will have to trust your senses and let your heart guide you!' Yousef stood upright and closed his eyes. The wind was getting stronger and blew the hot sand into his face. He had not been dressed for such a treacherous journey into the alien terrain. He had no choice but to carry on walking until it had passed. When it subsided, he opened his eyes again. In front of him he could see his street and his house. He shouted to his mother as she stood outside the house, but she looked right through him. Yousef turned around to see what she was looking at, and he saw his father walking towards her. He was smiling and waving, disguising the excruciating pain that he felt with every step. He was bent double, and his spine had a curvature that looked unnatural like the backs of the donkeys which were used for carrying and fetching on the Pharaoh's building sites. Both of his legs were bent outwards and looked close to buckling under his weight. His waving hands were blistered and calloused and he carried half a loaf of bread under his arm. Yousef had never really known his father, as he had died when he was only seven years old. His father along with his four brothers had been brought up the Nile with thousands of other like-minded people from rural areas to help build an empire, at the cost of their lives, as one by one, Yousef's four uncles had died, and in time, so did his father. The nomadic priest and his haunting sermon again had a related reading for such an occasion as this: 'Sometimes, in order for us to move forwards, we must release and let go of our past. What is done is done.' The mirage that was my past faded and disappeared. Yousef thought about his father's sacrifices, not for the empire, but for his family. A single teardrop rolled down his face and on to the sand, and from that single teardrop an oasis appeared out of the sand in front of him. It's just another mirage, Yousef thought to himself, and he was about to walk around it, when, out of the corner of his eye, he saw black silk waving in the breeze. He turned to see three very distinct figures. As his eyes adjusted, he was able to make out firstly a tall Bedouin, who was wearing the black silk cloak that had first caught his attention; he looked caring and compassionate, but warrior-like, and stood with his arms crossed. The second figure was of a short, round man, who he had seen on the temple steps that morning. And the third was the travelling priest, who had given a sermon outside the city that day. He watched as the three figures became one. I hope today has helped you to regain your identity and helped you to find yourself, bellowed the Bedouin figure, as it faded like a mirage into nothing. The oasis, however, was not a mirage, and after drinking from it and taking the shade offered by the palm trees which circled the welcoming pool of water, Yousef filled his water bottle, and started on his journey back to the city, which was now clearly visible and was no more than five miles away.

Wounded
Life is a battlefield;
and we are all the walking wounded!

Today, I will focus on,
the finding of and the reuniting of myself,
with who I really am.

Mother Earth, 'Who am I?'

Who am I and where did I come from?
Who decided that I would be me?
Who wrote my lifelong song?
The prejudices of others,
made me stand even stronger.
Life is like a stroll down a path,
a path which keeps getting longer.
I've never till now, had a place that I could call home,
and the long walk here,
I have made alone.
I've known all along who I am, don't you know;
I think that I just needed,
the right conditions to grow.

Those That Do

There are those amongst us,
who must travel,
because their souls
want them to see a special place,
before their time on earth comes to an end;
and then, there are those who travel,
because it is fashionable to do so.

When we resist change;
We resist our own growth!

On the Banks

I went down to the river; to secretly look,
at the place that I had read about: once, in a book.
Their clothes were in tatters, and they looked barely fed,
this couldn't be Utopia; my rose-coloured glasses turned red.
None of the stories I'd heard were true,
my dreams had been shattered, what would I do?
I looked down at the river, which was no longer blue.
Those scruffy little urchins, could well have been you.
I'll be back, I shout, as I turn around;
grateful for the distance, grateful for the ground.
When I tell my children,
that the grass isn't always greener;
I'd make them understand,
that they should be grateful that they live here,
and not in that other land.

Indigo Moonlight

If we want the children of our future to be led by our example,

then we really ought to make a start.

First of all we'll need the skills; to pass each one their part.

One by one they will realise their role; as small as it may seem,

they will as time goes by, all nations –

be a collective and work as one team.

I hope that our mistakes were there,

so that they could learn;

not to be repeated, as our children take their turn.

Goals

When we are young,

goals have to be met;

top of the class,

our future is set.

No room for error,

stick to the track,

when you make it to the age of sixteen,

only then you can look back.

Look at all your classmates,

why is it that they smile?

The chances are that it's because,

they were not pushed, that extra mile.

Another statistic, a temporary rise on a graph;

you mocked when you were young;

but it's them that have the last laugh.

It is in our darkest of hours,
those just before dawn,
that we are able to see the most!

A Routine of Infirmity

A blank moment;

staring nowhere,

a tremor in your hand,

and a thumping in your head.

A trip to the bathroom,

then turn around;

it's time to go back to bed.

Ripples

Ripples on a pond,

in a puddle,

bath tub,

or bowl of water;

are one of the few 'free,

easily emulated'

truly wondrous,

and beautiful

spectacles made available to us.

'Go on, try it.'

When pain was inflicted,

I felt pain;

when my heart was broken,

it hurt;

I think, 'therefore, I am.'

Knowledge

If you knew then,
half as much, as you know now;
you would have listened to your teachers,
as they taught you how,
'knowledge'
is mankind's most powerful tool;
knowing when to show it,
and when to play the fool.
A lack of knowledge,
will come back to haunt you,
as the questions in life,
baffle and taunt you.
There's a reason why words are written,
just as there is a reason why they are said;
it's so that the words that have meaning,
are the words that are left in your head.
Remember that knowledge can be gained,
just as knowledge can be abused,
it's up to you, the reader;
to decide how the knowledge is used.

Ignorance

Hate begins,
festers,
and grows,
out of all proportion
in the minds of ignorant men!
Who rarely remember,
their reasons for hating.

No Straight Lines

Nature chooses not to conform,
and has no perfectly straight lines;
or polygons of any size or shape:
no mathematical equations or formulations.
Then MAN happened,
'the rest', as we say, 'is history'.

The Global Playground

Is a belief worth killing another man for?

Is a line on a map worth killing another
man for?

No it isn't. So what's the problem?

In my humble opinion, it's over inflated
egos.

'Playground hierarchy, blown out of all
proportion.'

Only this time, it's not about conkers.

It's about bullets and guns.

It's also about which of the bullies, the
biggest bully is,

and which one has the most power, over all
the other kids.

A bully is a nobody; if nobody will do his
bidding, or his dirty work.

Everything happens for a reason;
even if it doesn't seem or feel like it at the time.

Awake

Yesterday
has come and gone,
everyone's asleep;
everyone, bar one.
He awaits the rising of the sun,
wishing his time away;
the minutes that make the hours,
and the hours that make the day.

If Only

If I could have my childhood back,
then that time would be happy and good.
I would make a point of understanding,
all of those things that were misunderstood.
I'd be aware of the consequences,
every time that I did wrong.
I'd let my family know I loved them,
before it's too late and they are all gone.
To all of the people, I did wrong,
I'd wipe the slate clean and undo;
I'd make peace with those people I'd wronged;
I'd make my peace with those I once
knew.

A moment lost, is a moment forever,
'you will never have it again'.
'Make each one count'.

The Bogey Man

I passed the 'Bogey Man' as I went to bed;
'I hope you've done all of your homework,'
the Bogey Man said.
'Excuse me', I replied,
as I pushed him out of the way,
'I'm not scared of you,
and it's not homework day'.

She Gave Me

She gave me music in my step,
she gave me a song in my heart,
I'll never hear the angels sing,
not now that we are apart.
There's no beat in my heart,
and there's no glint in my eye;
no more warm and glowing feeling,
from now until I die.

Poppy Day: Look Past the Tin

Their manners are impeccable;
they wear their berets and their medals with pride.
Homage paid, to those who never made it home,
in remembrance of those that died.
Remember the man who fought for us;
and remember his comrades that died;
then, look again, at the man in his beret –
and know why he wears it with pride.

Dress Rehearsal

SPORTS were always a preparation for WAR;

a macabre rehearsal for KILLING!

The bottom of a league table, is annihilation.

The top of a league division, is a supreme ruling.

There is no second, third, or fourth division,

And there is no weekend or casual local league.

Who can run the fastest, or jump the highest.

Throw or swim the furthest,

will always take the gold medal,

and will always win the war.

Within These Walls

The outer shell is crumbling, the walls now paper thin.

That which I held inside, I can no longer keep in.

My character is seeping out, on to the freezing-cold floor;

I was a fool to think that I would be safe, behind my impenetrable wall.

The screams that I thought came from elsewhere, were my own screams,

as they clawed their way out, those people that were the closest to me,

how did they not hear me shout? I find myself getting tired,

and desperate to get some sleep. The pain is becoming unbearable;

I feel scared, and I just want to weep.

Searching

She had wanted to know that she was on the right path to finding 'Spirit', although she had no doubts about the existence or the presence of it. Her life had been a testimony to what she believed, and through courses in healing, crystals and colour therapy, and more, as much as she knew that it came from within, she needed to 'see', she needed to 'feel', and she needed to have proof for herself; she thought that the answer had to be getting closer!

One day, whilst doing the usual things in town, she decided to go and have her 'tarot' cards read. It was usually a reading that would be taken with a pinch of salt, and not to be taken too seriously. The reading was booked for an hour's time, so she went to have a cup of tea in the town centre. Only the coffee shop that she normally frequented when in town, was no longer there. It had not been shut down, taken over or moved – it physically wasn't there; the building had gone! She looked around her and the only recognisable thing that she could see was the fountain in the middle of the square. Except, that is, for what could only be described as a small and quaint-looking taverna on the far side of the square, outside of which stood a tall and smartly dressed gentleman, with one arm folded at waist level, with a tea towel draped over it. With no other offer of refreshment, she walked over to the other side of the square, whereupon the smartly dressed waiter bowed. With his free hand, he gestured to her to pick a table at which to sit, as though the taverna was full, although there only seemed to be the two of them in town that day. The overly accommodating waiter then pulled out the chair for her and she sat down.

'Would madam care to see the menu?' he asked. 'Yes, I suppose she would,' she replied almost playfully. The waiter had a look about him that could have been mistaken for Mediterranean, but the accent was hard to make out at first – maybe mainland Europe with a mixture from more than the one country. As he turned to go back into the taverna, she caught a shimmer of gold that developed into a single large gold hoop earring. This made all of her earlier suspicions fall into place, and she surmised the waiter from the taverna that had appeared from nowhere was more than likely of Romany Gypsy origin, than an Essex lad out to impress. No more that a minute later, the waiter, who was obviously, it seemed at the time, hoping for a tip, re-emerged, with a full menu and a big smile. 'I was hoping for a nice pot of tea,' she said, almost apologetically. 'No problem, madam,' he graciously replied, before disappearing and reappearing with a pot of tea in one hand and a dainty little pot of milk in the other. Eager to please, he offered to pour the tea for her, which was just as eagerly declined. Without taking offence, he left her in peace and resumed his position of the dutiful servant, whom she had first seen from across the square. Not comfortable with this impertinent arrangement, on her behalf, she decided to strike up a conversation. 'Where do you and your family come from?' she asked, at the risk of sounding over presumptuous and nosy. 'I'm pleased you asked,' he replied, as though he had read her thoughts. 'My family, and countless generations of my family before, are travellers. We are descendents of the original gypsies, and as such, I have had passed down the secrets that only I can see, as has been the legacy bestowed upon the firstborn son of the family of the firstborn son of his. And as such, the family name and its secrets will never die; with any luck,' he said, with a cheeky, dimpled smile. 'For example,' he continued, 'I am able to tell your future, in many of the ways that others can for the price of a short learning course, or for the even cheaper cost of a book – which will apparently have all the answers within its shiny covers. Answers which have only come to myself, through countless generations, and I still have much to learn.' Her eyes looked downwards in shame. She had been made to feel for the first time as though all of the work she had put into finding her true calling had not brought her any closer to spirit; in fact, it had only served to confuse the messages and answers that she had spent her entire adult life looking for. 'Thank you,' she said, as she looked up at the waiter. 'You wanted to see, and now you have. Look from the inside out, rather than the other way around, try to calm yourself, after all a ship cannot get from one port to another, if the water is choppy or being bombarded with sleet and rain. You need to relax your mind, body and soul so you will be able to digest the real information, information that, that just is, and has not been written about, yet is very real.' She looked down at the floor again and lost herself in thought for a minute or two. When she lifted her head, just as she had half expected, the town square was teeming with life and she was once again sat outside her usual café, with no sign of the taverna or the gypsy waiter. The crying babies and all of the usual noises that would put her on edge, and the crowds that would have made her want to scream, had no effect on her as she walked back to where her car had been parked, filled with the realisation of what life was all about. She felt content with what she had been shown that day, and smiled to herself as she strolled down the high street. Then, like a bolt out of the blue, a group of three lads, who had obviously been drinking, bumped in to her, nearly knocking her off her feet. Then, just as she was about to hurl abuse at them, a glimmer of gold caught her eye, as the young man to which it was attached turned around and smiled at her.

Doubt

Have I made a difference?

I doubt it; not that you can see.

Below the surface though,

I have done my best; and that is all that matters to me.

Angry

The angry soul amongst us all,

sits crouching; lurking, waiting to pounce;

with its lips pulled back and bearing its gums,

salivating and with fangs glimmering, it then lunges forward,

sinking its teeth into the jugular vein of the unsuspecting

passer-by,

because they caused offence unknowingly.

'Nobody likes an angry soul; so find a reason to be happy.'

An over generous friend, is often an enemy in disguise!

Rank & File

A willingness and an acceptance 'to die' for one's country,

actually means, a willingness and an acceptance, 'to kill' for one's country –

somewhere inbetween lies an acceptance, 'to fight' for one's country.

To watch all that is around you fall,
and then to stand up tall and protest;
a Court Marshall will decide,
your fate quivers in their hands:
cowardice the verdict,
turn and face the wall.
A volley of shots and you died.

March On

The Trumpets lie still, the Drums and Pipes all gone.
Soldier boy looks up to the flag,
but in his heart he hears no song.
March on soldier boy; whilst the flag in front is flying,
March on soldier boy March On.
The flag in front is falling, the bearer lies hurt and dying,
Soldier boy picks it up; the flag again is flying.

Limbo

Welcome to limbo,
halfway in between;
a million lifetimes of nothing,
an eternity never seeing.
If you're lucky,
the living,
will help you to walk into the light.
If not,
you will spend forever here;
where every day
is every night.

A War Without Reason

The nation was in uproar,
we could not let it be.
So our army was sent to war,
our air force to the skies,
and the navy was put to sea.
The dictatorship was toppled,
the people at last free;
the day we went to war;
over land and air and sea.
Then it started to branch off:
north, east, south and west;
A very different war,
but our forces did their best.
It seems like we can't loose face,
or we can't be seen to give in.
A war that will last forever,
a war we cannot win.

Materialism – all of our stuff and our things,
bank statements, pay rolls, and the anguish it all brings.
A pocket full of nothing, and the wide open road;
no heavy burden, and no heavy load.
Happy that you answer only to you,
and happy that you decide where to go and what you do.

Alone in my Darkness

Alone in my darkness,
with no human contact;
my friends are all gone,
the hours all strung together,
making my days seem so long.
I wear a watch to keep an ever-watchful eye on the
time;
which stretches,
distorts and turns a full circle on itself,
devouring that which was,
to tell a new time.
In my endless dark sorrow,
I nervously watch the second hand,
as it gradually, slowly
and inevitably reaches tomorrow.

Haley's Big Brother

I flew through the air, with power and grace,
wondering which new challenge I'd face.
All of the others I'd left in rubble,
this one looked weak, and not much trouble.
I'd wondered if they would see me come,
When, like a bolt out of the blue,
I circled their sun.
Not giving them time
to put their plans into play,
I hurtled towards them; Armageddon Day.
As I got closer, I took a look to see;
that they'd been destroying themselves,
they didn't need me.
I took a new course,
back out to space,
a fleeting look back, just in case.
That was the only time,
that I can safely say,
that a planet turned against itself,
and scheduled its own doomsday.

White Elephants

Made from ivory,
and thought to bring good luck.
On a key ring,
in a pocket,
a handbag or a purse.
People and their things,
were the elephants' curse.

The Gardener

He was just a gardener; but one whose passion for the fruits of harvest, was like that of no other man or gardener I had ever met. I remember asking him on more than one occasion, why was it that he had no tools other than his hands; and he would only ever answer with a smile. One day I decided to watch from a distance to satisfy my own curiosity. He fetched the wheelbarrow from the shed, took off his hat and mopped his brow; poured himself a coffee from his flask; and set about reading the newspaper which he had brought with him; then he made himself comfortable under the large sycamore tree and fell asleep. Infuriated at the cheek of the man, I went over to confront him. As I reached the snoring gardener, I looked over at the wheelbarrow and noticed it was full of brambles and weeds. Then I noticed that the gardener had one eye open, watching my confusion, bewilderment and utter disbelief at what I had seen. He slowly got up from the floor, dusted himself off, adjusted his hat and asked, 'Did you really think that I was working on my own?'

The Day I Left Home

Only young and wide-eyed I looked back to see, the home that I'd left, and the life that was me; with a suitcase full of hope, a heart full of dreams, and a future I'd find in no book, I walked along an all too familiar path, but a whole new direction it took. I'd learn so much about the world in which I live, I'd learn what it was that I should hold on to, and I'd learn that which was free to give; the sun shone for me that day, as I walked into a future not set. I hoped it would continue to shine down on me, and for my story which was not written yet.

Royal Mail

The postman's bicycle stopped outside, and brought news to my mother that my father had died.

The ultimate sacrifice made, but I'll never know why he had gone so far from his home to die. My mother's tears should never have been spilled; my dad should have stayed at home, and he should never have been killed. A guard of honour and a 21-gun salute, as my father lay cold, in his very best suit. Everybody had a brave story to tell, stories about my father, of the day that he fell. Comforting words; but just 'words' that can't heal, this hole in my heart, and the sadness I feel. He doesn't sit at the table, or make us smile any more, ever since my dad went to the room through the door. 'Have a safe journey, Dad, because you have earned your wings, and I'll think of you every time a robin-redbreast sings.'

'And Now the Weather ...'

We watch the daily weather; but it would seem that we can't, or 'don't want' to understand;

how we've influenced the weather which now blights our green and pleasant land.

It could have been so different for the generations yet to come; they could have seen the beauty of winter, and they could have enjoyed the summer sun. As it is we leave them a world dishevelled, broken and burnt; and with a countless number of lessons, which our generation never learnt.

The Land of the Thistle

It was one of those days when not very much happens, unless you make it happen. It was a time of unrest, that even the clansmen of the Mctigue Clan had a foreboding feeling about. The clan's people were a warring clan and proud of it; and from the chieftain down to the smallest of children, they all knew of no other life; except for that day. The mothers were at home watching over the babies and the little ones, whilst the fathers had gone out hunting for deer; although with the exception of the face paint, they had left dressed for battle, agitated by the air of peace, and spoiling for a fight. Myself and the rest of my clan, who were between the ages of twelve and fifteen, had left the safety of the village boundaries and gone further than that which was deemed safe and allowed by our parents. On the subject of safety though, we were all armed with wooden swords and shields, that had been fashioned from off-cuts and remnants that had been thrown out after our fathers had added to their own shields, making them more resilient and resistant to a sword's blow in battle. My father had recently returned from one such battle, where all the clans had, for the first and last time, joined forces and stood up to the King of England and the so called King of Scotland. He had returned brandishing a Claymore sword, which he had taken as a trophy from an English officer, and the ownership of such a sword had given him a promotion of sorts, and my mother and I subsequently enjoyed the tribal rise in status. As had I within my miniature tribe been awarded a promotion; and I was now in charge of the younger, more aspiring chieftains; some of whom had only just qualified to join our mini Mctigue clan. Nevertheless, what they lacked in stature they made up for by a hundred times in gumption and an eagerness to learn. As ridiculous as our mini clan may sound, for as long as our clan has been, the children have always prepared themselves for adulthood via mini Mctigue clans, wooden swords and shields, made from scraps of leather and fur discarded by their fathers. Our fathers would all gather at times, and watch as the older children taught the youngsters how to fight and to use a sword. The young clan would

gather on the brow of the hill, with sword in one hand and shield in the other – the next generation of warriors, each of them ready to kill. In the distance they could see another army – like them – willing to fight to the death for their family, clan and glen. We ran down into the valley, as did they, our wooden swords and shields clashed, but no blood was spilt that day. Full of bruises and splinters, they all sat on the ground, with their new friends that Fate had found. They were no different, so why had they been brought up with hatred and killing in mind? They all made a pact that day, at the foot of the hill: one day, when all grown into men, they would meet at the foot of the hill again. But that day never came. I grew up and took up arms against the other clans, and I took more lives than I care to remember, in the countless battles that took place over hunting grounds and glens. Sometimes I go back to the very same hill that we had charged down all those years ago; where we fought those who became our friends; and I think about the pact that we made but never kept. I wonder if they do the same! Maybe one day our paths will cross again, and maybe we'll sit on the ground, and laugh together, about the day we went home with our hands full of splinters, and not covered in the blood of our fellow countrymen.

Once we find ourselves on the right path, our destiny will unfold, and we will attract others in our soul group, and together we will accomplish (that which we came here to do)!

Surplus

We don't appreciate what we've got until it's gone, as Mark was to find out the hard way. His life had been full of training at the gym, nights of drunken revelry, and days which consisted of a blatant disrespect for the ladies, who were able to put up with him and his lifeless lifestyle, for more than one night. Then, one day, one week, one month – who knows – he was stopped in his tracks. It's irrelevant how, or why; its only importance is that it probably stopped him from ending up in an early and very lonely grave. All of a sudden, he was unable to do all the things that he was used to doing. It was time for him to regroup, reanalyse, and re-evaluate his life, which he had trouble in doing. Everyone had advice and lists as long as his arm, of agendas, plans of action and foolhardy and inappropriate comparisons and goals. Everybody had an opinion on the path he should take and the direction he should follow; with the focus and emphasis being put on whatever he was still capable of doing; but he was more concerned about the things which he could no longer do. Mark just wanted nothing to do with anything or anybody, and he found himself living in his own hell, in which he was unable to walk away from the barrage of voices in his head, ears, and space – which was what the people he cared about had become. More times than he would care to remember, he had this crazy notion to end it all, but what kind of example would that have been to his children – what message would it have sent to them? He refused to put another dent in their self-worth and self-belief, as they became young adults. Even though they lived quite a distance away, and he didn't get to see them very often, they were always in his thoughts and his heart; his blood ran through their veins – as their blood ran through his. He would often find himself looking out of his window, looking at life. And in his most selfish of thoughts, would be those two words that came so easily, and were rarely considered important, that he would learn the most from: why me? The answer wasn't in him at that time, and nor was it in the books that he read. He came to the conclusion that apart from passing on his genes, he had no other purpose and was now surplus to requirements. Then one day, Mark woke up and opened his eyes; not to another dark day in hell, but to an awakening of himself, his soul and his life. He felt as though he had been punched in the stomach, his breathing was heavy and laboured, and his head was spinning. He felt disembodied from himself, at first just for a moment at a time out of sequence, and then for five to ten seconds at a time, or at least that was how it seemed to Mark. Everything around him began to exist in a synchronised time, as if a gigantic metronome had been started; and the light in his bedroom was so bright that it hurt his eyes, as though he was looking directly at the sun. After enduring all of these things for what seemed like an age, but was probably more like only a few seconds, it all fell into line and the feeling that he had remaining was that of warmth and serenity from within. When he looked up at the ceiling to see the blinding light, all he saw was his lampshade swinging gently, as though a moth had landed on it, and no light at all; the light switch had been, and still was, in the off position. It was a while longer before his breathing and head returned to a more natural state. Nothing seemed real any more; it was as though he had been on a fairground ride. His legs were shaky and as he made his way to the kitchen, his feet felt as though they were sinking into the floor. On reaching the kitchen, he felt neither hungry nor thirsty, so he turned around and trudged his way through to the living room. He sat on the setee and leant across to retrieve the television remote control. He couldn't get a signal on the TV, and all the usual channels were unobtainable; except for one, which was a hospital programme televising a live operation. The patient had been in a high-speed road accident, in which he was the only survivor out of the four young men in the vehicle, which had hit the centre reservation whilst travelling at between one hundred and one hundred and ten miles per hour. It had then flipped on to its roof and crossed over the reservation into the path of on-coming traffic, none of whom were involved, thankfully, or so it seemed at first; the car that the patient was travelling in had veered over towards the grass verge and disappeared. Several cars pulled over on to the hard shoulder. The television switched itself off, and continued to play in his head. Mark could hear all the voices and screams, his head was spinning round and around; he could remember calling out to his friends and hearing no reply. In fact, he had heard nothing at all for the remaining part of the rescue. Eventually, the spinning slowed down before total darkness came over him, like the heavy velvet curtains swooping in at the end of a stage production; in which he had played the lead, in an all-too-familiar plot. He tried to reach the light, but he'd been turned away. His friends turned around, and said, 'Be strong, we'll meet again some day.' Six weeks later, he woke up in his hospital bed, trying to make sense of what all the doctors said. He often went to the graveyard, and would see a young lady, who went to take flowers for her husband and her baby. They would talk about the bright light into which they both had wanted to go. It turned out that the event that had brought them both such great pain, had been interwoven, they were one and the same. He knew now why he'd been left behind, to offer comfort to the lady that he would one day find. For the next thirty years, their friendship stood strong, in memory of friends, and the family who were gone.

Wonders

Moon beams, and sunrays,
and all of the clouds in between,
nature's many wonders;
the wonders I have seen.
I watch the doves of peace as they elegantly fly,
just one of God's many creatures,
that came to earth from the sky!

My Harrogate

Harrogate was the place where I did my growing up;
barely out of school and taking charge of my life,
I left home and I became me.
Some of the choices that I made,
weren't the best, but they were mine.
Now a lot of the decisions that I make aren't mine at all;
and sometimes I feel as though I never left home,
and I never made that step into that which was unknown.
I will now and for the rest of my days,
look out on to the world,
through my window,
that looks on to my Harrogate.

Don't Cry

You tell your children,
that you'll no longer be there,
and you wipe away their tears;
but who will be there when you're drowning in yours,
throughout all of your lonely years?

The Cairngorms

As a young man I encountered the Cairngorms' snow-covered mountain peaks of the Scottish Highlands, and I came to appreciate the planet's glacial age; a time in mankind's early history. A time when the priority was surviving the day, and hunting was a necessity, not a lifestyle choice, and never a sport. To make an igloo, or to dig an ice hole into the mountainside, to call on instincts suppressed by time and evolution, and to pitch my skills against those of one of the planet's harshest environments, and yet one of its most beautiful.

Take some time out, to sit and wonder, and to put your life into perspective, (it will be time well spent).

Nightmares

Call it what you like, purgatory, hell, or limbo,
it's the damp, dark place of nightmares;
it's a place you don't want to go!

Hit & Run

The hit and run driver, hit me and my friend,
she fell to the floor as the car sped around the bend.
He could have killed her, only thirteen,
yet the life that lay in front of her,
was a life she would not have seen.
The act of a stranger, with no regard for another's life,
could have denied a child a mother,
and could have denied a husband a wife.

The Pages in the Book

A book never opened is a waste of paper, and the wasted life of a
tree, so starving our planet of essential gases, and the habitat of
many different creatures. Open the book, even if only to feel and
appreciate the leaves of paper (the pages) that lie between the hard
and decorative covers, or if only to thank our planet for its sacrifice.
If you don't think that you can do this; then pass the book on to
somebody who can.

In order to walk the path you must first become the path,
taking on its direction in order to discover its destination.

Déjà Vu

You go to a town, to which you've never seen,

you know your way around the streets,

to which you have never been;

déjà vu which you can't explain,

you know the person who just walked past you,

but you don't know their name.

There are things out there that in this incarnation we
will never know;

things beyond the void,

which our universe chooses not to show.

The human heart is a door, that can only be opened from the inside,
with a key that can only be given and shared by you. Guard it well,
you only have the one (and it can't be bought). When it has been
broken, the cracks will   not always show at a glance; though its
vulnerabilities will weaken your resolve. Making it an easy prey, for
those who will take pleasure from your torment.

A moment lost,
is a moment lost forever,
you will never have it again.
Make each one count.

My Lot

I put my hand in my pocket, hoping that maybe I had some small amount of loose change that had maybe hidden and eluded my daily rummage in the creases and folds of material; I opened my fist, and found my palm was empty. It had been a pointless exercise as I had already known the outcome; and one which would be repeated daily. I put my hands back in my pockets, and carried on walking. It was a grey day (even greyer than usual), and the sky was filled with heavy sagging clouds that looked ready to burst at any moment. I pulled the collar of my jacket up and concertinaed my neck downwards, whilst raising my shoulders into a permanent shrug, a very clever sequence of actions that comes so natural to us all. I pursed my lips; and whistled an out-of-tune ditty, which I was hoping would distract my attention away from my cold, grey and penniless situation (it never did, but I would do it anyway). I knew my way to the soup kitchen with my eyes closed and whilst walking backwards. As I approached it I was welcomed by several familiar faces, those which were there every morning; just as I was. Hygiene standards aside, you would be hard pressed to find anyone (of the working or the upper classes, that is) with such a smile, and happy outlook on life, even after it had turned its back on them. The doors opened and the staff exchanged morning salutations with the orderly line of hungry and grateful gentlemen; a hot cup of tea, and a hearty breakfast of sausages, baked beans, fried eggs and toast, was something that I and others in my position welcomed with all our hearts; and we even discussed politics, the state of the country, and other topics of current affairs. Then the kitchen staff would ask us politely to leave, and said that they looked forward to seeing us the following morning. We would meander towards the park before saying goodbye until the next day. I wandered off in the direction of the high street and then over the main road and on to the bank of the canal, where I headed towards the cover provided by the bridge, and sat down on the path, the only place for me to shelter from both the cold, and the judgemental gazes of those whom I would once have called my neighbours, my work colleagues and my friends. My lot isn't most people's idea of a happy lot; but I would have to differ, because this is my happy lot.

'Twas a Good Year

The rosy-cheeked ladies said goodbye to their men;

time to harvest the fields had soon come around again.

The work hands were in the fields before the sun was awake,

they were soon put to work, they had bales to make.

The wheat was chaffed,

and the land was tilled;

tables were laden,

and larders were filled.

After the harvest there was always a fair,

with plenty to eat, and cider to share.

It never seemed the same in the years to follow;

it all became modern, it all became hollow.

Tractors, balers and greedy city folk,

gone were the days of the ox and the yoke.

Nostalgic images no longer seen,

a way of life, which once had been.

In Summary

I am no more a Christian than I am a Muslim; a Buddhist; or any of the other religions that dominate the social, moralistic demographics of the world. Neither am I an atheist, as I do believe that there is something after this life, or all of my learning will have been in vain; and the mistakes I have made, will have served no other purpose than to make me disappointed with myself for having failed 'again'. Whatever awaits me when I pass over to the other side, I want to arrive with my head held high; proud of the life I had; proud of who I am, and who I have been; and having learnt the lessons which I came here to learn.

MY MESSAGE TO YOU – Be nice and be true to yourself, try to never let your light fade, become dim, or extinguish and die.